CONFRONTING A CONTROLLING GOD

A *Confronting Fundamentalism* Book

CONFRONTING A CONTROLLING GOD

CHRISTIAN HUMANISM AND THE MORAL IMAGINATION

CATHERINE M. WALLACE

CASCADE *Books* · Eugene, Oregon

CONFRONTING A CONTROLLING GOD
Christian Humanism and the Moral Imagination

A Confronting Fundamentalism Book

Cascade Books
An Imprint of Wipf and Stock Publishers
199 W. 8th Ave., Suite 3
Eugene, OR 97401

www.wipfandstock.com

Paperback ISBN 978-1-4982-2893-0
Hardcover ISBN 978-1-4982-2895-4
Ebook ISBN 978-1-4982-2894-7

Cataloging-in-Publication data

Names: Wallace, Catherine M.

Title: Confronting a controlling god: Christian humanism and the moral imagination / Catherine M. Wallace.

Description: Eugene, OR: Cascade Books, 2016 | Series: Confronting Fundamentalism | Includes bibliographical references.

Identifiers: ISBN 978-1-4982-2893-0 (paperback) | ISBN 978-1-4982-2895-4 (hardcover) | ISBN 978-1-4982-2894-7 (ebook)

Subjects: 1. Christianity and justice. 2. Good and evil. I. Theodicy. Title.

Classification: BJ1401 .W27 2016 (print) | BJ1401 (ebook)

Manufactured in the USA.

Grateful acknowledgment is made to Marie Howe and W. W. Norton to reprint "Annunciation," from *The Kingdom of Ordinary Time*, copyright © 2008 by Marie Howe (New York: W. W. Norton, 2008). Reprinted by permission of W. W. Norton & Company, Inc. All rights reserved.

for Aislin Grace Wallace and Adelia Wren Wallace,
to whom the future belongs

Table of Contents

Preface

Thanks for picking up this book. After so many years of solitary work, it's thrilling to welcome a reader. I'm delighted you are here, and I hope you find what you are looking for. I look forward to hearing from you when you are finished reading: drop me a line at my website, CatherineMWallace.com, and, if you'd like, follow me on Facebook (CatherineMWallaceBooks) and Twitter (@ Cate_Wallace).

This book stand on its own, completely self-contained. But it's also part of a larger conversation, a book series called *Confronting Fundamentalism*. In each of these other books I focus on a specific objection to fundamentalism: it's anti-gay; antiscience; literal-minded and absolutist; judgmental and bullying. Perhaps most seriously, fundamentalist support for torture and capital punishment resonates with Christianity's dark history of complicity in political violence: crusades, inquisitions, pogroms, and the myriad abuses of colonialism. That history raises a major question: *is God violent?* The God proclaimed by Jesus was not. Jesus was intransigently clear on that point: God loves everyone. God smites no one, not now and not in the afterlife.

You can read the first chapters of these other books on my website. In each of them, issue by issue, I lay out some aspect of two concepts that I hope will become part of a new conversation among reasonable, politically moderate, critical-thinking Americans. The first concept is *humanism,* an intellectual and moral tradition going

back to the fourteenth century. Some of us are Christian humanists; some of us are secular humanists. Some of us are humanists
in other religious traditions. Some of us simply believe in morality
and human decency even though we answer "none of the above"
when some pollster tries to sort us into a specific tradition. To be
a *humanist*, I contend, is to share two major commitments. First,
we are committed to *the humane* as a moral standard. Second, we
are committed to critical thinking and the honest use of language
as intellectual standards. If we have a name for what we have in
common, we can far more easily network with one another. We are
all *humanists*.

Furthermore, living up to these two commitments demands
a cognitive and creative ability properly called *the moral imagination*. That's the second concept I offer to help delineate the common ground underneath our feet. Imagination properly defined
is the cognitive ability to grapple with paradox. It's the ability to
recognize and work with the frameworks, paradigms, and models
that inform critical thinking and successful problem-solving at all
levels. The problem with fundamentalism, by contrast, is that it's
both painfully literal-minded and intransigently rigid. It's incapable
of creative problem-solving.

Christian humanism and the moral imagination together
paint a very different portrait of God from what Christian fundamentalism proclaims. Fundamentalism portrays God as massively
controlling. They use that portrait to legitimate their own control
needs and to drape in pseudo-religious legitimacy a reactionary,
libertarian political agenda that has nothing whatsoever to do with
what Jesus taught. Jesus proclaimed a very different God—a God
experienced as dynamic, compassionate Presence. In this volume, I
take a look at what's involved in rescuing the God of Jesus from the
clutches of the Religious Right.

I'm not trying to convert anyone. I believe an immensely valuable cultural heritage is at risk no less decisively than statues of the
Buddha blown up by the Taliban or ancient temples demolished by
ISIS. I hope to offer insight that you don't have to become Christian
to admire, just as you don't have to become Buddhist to admire

Buddhist insight. To paraphrase the Dalai Lama, the point here is not becoming Christian. The point is becoming wise.

And the wisdom we need most right now is the wisdom to reclaim the common ground that we share. We have gotten here from many directions, guided by many moral traditions. That diversity should be a source of strength and vitality, just as our ethnic diversity should be. It will be, it can be, if reasonable and informed people speak up. *And listen to one another.*

I'm honored by your willingness to listen to me. Thanks for being here.

Acknowledgements

In the decade I spent working on this book and others like it, I was repeatedly cheered on by generous audiences and critical readers. I owe a lot to these good people and to the local congregations or civic organizations that invited me to speak. These audiences read or listened patiently as I struggled to get my thinking in order and my sources under control. They patiently endured academic digressions that I later deleted. They convinced me that the world is full of open-minded, compassionate, morally sensitive people who delight in the quirky facts of cultural history.

Above all, they influenced my writing in quite remarkable ways. They insisted that my stories about my own experience are crucial and so I should tell more of them. One evening I worried aloud that this storytelling was distracting. Didn't it disrupt the flow of my argument?

"Look," one woman insisted sharply, "that's how I know it's an important point. You stop and tell a story." Everyone else nodded. Well, okay then. Stories. The more stories I told, the more often audiences told me that the stories were crucial.

Audiences also gave me permission to restate classical issues in philosophy or theology using very down-to-earth language. During discussion after my presentation, I'd reframe some complicated issue with an "it's like this" analogy. *Say that,* people would insist. *Just say that. Why didn't you just say that in the first place?* Let me tell you why: I was haunted by the Ghost of Professors Past, that's why. In time I banished that ghost. (Well, mostly.) I could never have done so without their flat-out and repeated insistence that they wanted to hear this more immediate, more vulnerable voice.

And that's not all. They convinced me I had to keep going. Their raw anger and bitter frustration kept me at my desk. I realized that there are a lot of us—Christian humanists and secular humanists alike—who sharply oppose the hard Right, highly politicized misappropriation of Christianity. Lots of people are eager for the backstory and the alternatives that I have to offer. They don't have the time to read all the stuff that I've read, and furthermore they don't have the scholarly background some of my sources presuppose. But they are just as curious and just as passionate as I am. They were as happy to find me as I've been to find a good plumber, or a competent tax guy, or a clever app. We need one another's skills.

In my audiences were Christians who are angry that the Christian "brand" has lost all connection to Jesus of Nazareth. They want their religion back. They want their God back. They are seriously pissed that "Christian" has come to mean "ignorant bigot," even though they understand that perception.

In my audience were people whose alienation from Christianity arose from how much they have read about Western political history. They argued powerfully that Christianity has often been guilty of encouraging violence, enabling violence, and taking direct violent action itself. I knew these facts as well as they did. But the moral passion of their repudiation of Christianity on this basis forced me into taking a hard look at the theological justifications that were offered at the time. That in turn elicited a far clearer, far more direct statement of my own theological position.

In my audiences were secular humanists. Some are outraged by encounters with "church people." Their stories haunt me. Some are outraged by the transparently anti-intellectual and theocratic ambitions of the radical Religious Right. They are offended by claims that this is a "Christian" nation and so one narrow version of Christianity should be allowed to usurp the law of the land and the democratic process. Many secular humanists are of course ex-Christians: some rejected a rigid, judgmental, anti-intellectual hard

Right religiosity, which was the only version of Christianity available to them.

Others were religiously unaffiliated. They had drifted away from dysfunctional congregations or from a faith that felt self-absorbed, irrelevantly dogmatic, and remote from the actual moral issues confounding daily life. Still others had tough and honest questions that had been dodged by clergy or by Sunday school teachers. That was that, as far as they were concerned. I have to respect anyone who takes religion seriously enough to reject incoherent versions.

Across the board I was honored by how people angry at or alienated from Christianity nonetheless listened to me. They listened willingly; they listened openly. They realized I'm not trying to convert anybody. I was honored by their trust on that point. But they pushed hard, asking terrific questions and holding their ground when I pushed back. That process helped me clarify my thinking. It helped me understand my primary audience, which *is* secular humanists.

Some in my audiences have belonged to other faith traditions. These people were often quite eloquent about what they have found and why they value it. That too was invaluable. It helped me to find a conceptual language sufficiently open to communicate broadly.

And I'm pleased to acknowledge publicly how much I have treasured the warm encouragement and invaluable help with Greek, Latin, and Hebrew offered by T. Gerald Jansen. He is a priest in the Anglican Church of Canada, an emeritus Professor of Old Testament at Christian Theological Seminary, Indianapolis, and a very fine Coleridge scholar besides. I'm not a biblical scholar no matter how broadly you want to define that term. Gerry is. I don't mean to poach his prestige: what I do with the Moses scene remains entirely my responsibility. But as you will see for yourself when you get to chapter 8, there are some fascinating technical issues in how that scene has been translated.

Late in the process, I discovered major public affirmation of conversations like the ones I'd been having for ten years. In April 2014, Brookings issued a report, *Faith in Equality,* calling on Christian political progressives to reach out both to secular political progressives and to politically progressive religious conservatives for whom "Christianity" still has a clear theological connection to what Jesus actually taught about inclusivity, the image of God in everyone, and social justice as delineated by the great Jewish prophets. I take this report as evidence that the tide is turning nationally in opposition to hard Right reactionaries in the Christian tradition.

I'm delighted to be part of that. I'm even more delighted to feel that I am speaking both to and for a solid core of ordinary, moderate, religiously tolerant Americans.

Grace and peace be with us all.

1

Confronting Fundamentalism: The Dangerous God of "Control and Condemn"

Christian fundamentalism speaks for God with breathtaking arrogance and sweeping authority, laying out in no uncertain terms what God demands and whom God condemns. For instance, God demands that all schools officially endorse Christianity by having public prayer and Bible reading. God condemns geology and evolutionary biology and now, it seems, climate science. Strictly speaking, theologically speaking, such claims are a variety of *idolatry*. They are the result of unskillful theology that puts something else in place of God. Specifically, here, fundamentalism deifies and then worships human control needs inflated to the cosmic level. Fundamentalism proclaims and worships this idol in an effort to legitimate a reactionary political and social agenda. That agenda is diametrically opposed to what Jesus taught and what Jesus inherited from the Jewish prophetic tradition before him.

Their God of radical control needs is the product of Christian theocracy in the West—the thousand years in which Christianity was the established religion of the Roman Empire and its successors. As I explain in *Confronting Religious Violence*, chapter 3, the political function of religion in a theocracy is to serve as the public relations organization of the emperor or the king. Theocracy is

1

never about putting religion directly in charge of the state: spiritual enlightenment (by whatever name) cannot be imposed by force of law. The name of the game in a theocracy is using religious language and symbolism to legitimate the authority of whoever holds power—or seeks power.

And so, Christian fundamentalism does not seek the just, humane, inclusive society preached by Jesus of Nazareth. It offers "religious" cover to a political agenda that is sharply opposed to democratic government of the people, by the people, and for the people. For secular reactionaries, the price of collaborating with Christian fundamentalism has been endorsing policies and legislation attempting to impose "Christian morality" upon the nation as a whole. In *God's Own Party: The Making of the Christian Right* (2010), historian Daniel Williams points out that alliance with secular reactionaries offered religious reactionaries something they had never had before: an economic agenda (radical *lassez faire* predatory capitalism) and a foreign policy agenda (aggressively militaristic "neocon" imperialism). This complex and somewhat contradictory alliance made it possible for the Religious Right to make a major play for control of the Republican Party. That's the story Williams tells in scholarly detail in what began as his doctoral dissertation at Brown.

In his book *In God We Trust: How Corporate America Invented Christian America* (2015), Princeton historian Kevin Kruse describes how this alliance began. It began in the 1930s, he explains, as an initiative by major business leaders opposed to such New Deal developments as Social Security, unemployment insurance, banking regulations, and labor reform. They wanted to undermine the New Deal and to shore up the reputation of the banking industry, which was widely condemned for its role in the Great Depression. And so they began channeling money to right-wing clergy who thought that the New Deal was "unbiblical." Kruse documents this process in rigorous scholarly detail from its origin in the 1930s and 1940s through the merger of piety, patriotism, and reactionary politics in the 1950s.

In *With God on Our Side: The Rise of the Religious Right in America* (2005), Rice University historian William Martin continues the tale Kruse tells. Martin documents the arc of fundamentalism from the mid-1950s through the end of the twentieth century, focusing on opposition to civil rights: racial equality, gender equality, reasonable freedom of conscience for women regarding their own healthcare, and the separation of church and state generally. In denouncing civil rights legislation and Supreme Court decisions assuring civil rights, the Religious Right repeated arguments first made in opposition to the New Deal: such initiatives were "intrusive government regulations" disrupting "the American way" and "our way of life." Government itself was declared the enemy, the beast that must be starved into submission—by electing candidates who would defund regulatory agencies, and cut taxes on businesses and the wealthiest households (that's how this alliance operated).

As Rice explains, the Religious Right provided to the radically libertarian, anti-government political Right something it had never had before: extensive grassroots support, local political networks, and above all people willing to vote against the economic interests of their own families and communities. Slick, theologically dishonest manipulation has slowly turned this complex alliance on the hard Right into a major threat to American democratic traditions and processes.

Whether the "Republican establishment" can regain control from this alliance has become a very open question. They need to, because as Daron Acemoglu (MIT) and James Robinson (Harvard) explain in *Why Nations Fail* (2012), strong central government and appropriate "level playing field" regulations are essential to entrepreneurial opportunity and a vital economy making good use of people's talents and hard work. For example, carbon emissions regulations of some sort have broad support in the business community, where smart and morally responsible executives realize that this is necessary. But it will be expensive, and only wise legislation can ensure that environmentally responsible companies are not penalized. This is common sense—desperately needed common sense. But common sense is not politically viable because climate change denial has been widely advocated by this devastating alliance between fundamentalist religious reactionaries and radically libertarian economic reactionaries.

This alliance is responsible for acute dysfunction in Washington and for the commonplace spectacle of wildly contra-factual and irresponsible political grandstanding to the fundamentalist "Republican" base. We all know that. What too few people appreciate fully is the straight *theological* illegitimacy of this fundamentalism. Specifically, the controlling God of fundamentalism is a dangerous illusion. Such theology, if I can dignify it with that label, is a malignant development within Christian tradition. As I have explained elsewhere in the *Confronting Fundamentalism* series, the God proclaimed by the Religious Right is perhaps best understood as a "modernist" distortion of authentic Christian theology.[1] The distortion was most notable or most extreme in the US, because the controlling and punitive God was famously embraced by the Puritans.[2]

As Charles Taylor documents at great length in *A Secular Age* (2007), the West began to reject Christianity and to move toward secularism not because people preferred science to religion, but rather because there is something both morally repugnant and unconvincing about this hyper-controlling and vindictive God. In *God's Problem* (2008), biblical scholar Bart Ehrman does a fine job of exploring the moral problems attendant upon a controlling God. He concludes that God does not exist and Christianity is false, because the only God he can imagine is a God in absolute causal control of everything.

I'd reply to Ehrman that the God of Jesus cannot be defined as control over causality. Christian humanism as I understand it makes that claim with great confidence and on the basis of generations of rigorous scholarship. Strictly speaking, Christian humanism is the genuinely *biblical* and *conservative* tradition here. Fundamentalism—Protestant and Catholic alike—is a dangerous Victorian brew of theological nonsense and political expediency. I delineate

---

1. I explain fundamentalism as a modernist distortion in *Confronting Religious Denial of Science*, chapter 5, and again in passing in *Confronting Religious Absolutism*, chapter 5

2. I discuss the Puritans and the Great Awakenings in *Confronting Religious Judgmentalism*, chapter 10.

its origins from many different perspectives in other volumes of the *Confronting Fundamentalism* series.

I believe that we need to reclaim an older and very different set of ideas about who God is. That's one way to confront fundamentalism. It's not the only way. But it's a start, and it is perhaps the most effective way of confronting them: other Christians are best situated to deny fundamentalism the religious legitimacy and the powerful cultural capital it tries to exploit.

Consider this: radical misappropriations of Islam can only be stopped if other Muslims speak up clearly *and get an audience* when they say, "that's not Islam." Similarly, Christian fundamentalism is not Christianity. It does not represent the teachings of Jesus—nor the faith of millions of American Christians, including plenty of educated, thoughtful evangelicals.

What's at Stake Today

How God is defined or understood should matter *even to nonbelievers* because extraordinarily powerful cultural capital is at stake. These resources must not fall into the wrong hands. To whatever extent that has already happened, it behooves all humanists—regardless of our religious affiliation or non-affiliation—to recognize and oppose this misappropriation. In *God and Empire: Jesus against Rome Then and Now* (2007), biblical scholar John Dominic Crossan explains why. He argues forcefully that fundamentalist Christianity is in fact a far more dangerous threat to the global future than fundamentalist Islam. Here's the issue as I have come to see it: Christianity has completely lost control of its brand. Pope Francis may be trying to reclaim it; but the odds are against him, just as the odds are stacked again politically progressive, theologically sophisticated mainline Protestant denominations.

Let me explain what's at stake in Christianity losing control of its brand. Here's the threat: fundamentalism is dangerous in part because Christian symbolism permeates Western culture. Both consciously and unconsciously, both visibly and in deeply submerged or coded ways, Christianity shapes archetypal Western narratives and our most powerful cultural images. You don't need a degree in marketing to recognize how potent such resources can be. Brands are stories, marketing folks insist. And at the core of the brand story is a compelling image. Christian stories and images provide some of the most potent symbolism in Western culture.

In particular, how we define God reveals or provides the cultural source code for how we understand ourselves. The medieval church called this the "*imitatio dei*," the "imitation of God." That is, we are called to imitate God to the best of our limited human ability. Who God is—the identity of God—thus delineates what we can legitimately expect of ourselves and what we can legitimately demand of one another. That expectation can lead us spiritually in two very different directions depending upon how we define God.

First, the "power of God" can be defined spiritually and morally as the transforming power of compassion, generosity, and hospitality. If that's how we think of God, then our theology leads us spiritually to trust in compassion, to endeavor to cultivate compassion in ourselves, and so forth. Or as the prophet Micah said in 700 BCE or so:

> He has showed you, O man, what is good;
> and what does THE LORD require of you
> but to do justice, and to love kindness,
> and to walk humbly with your God? (Mic 6:8, RSV)

That's the tradition I'm referring to here when I say that Christian humanism is the genuinely *conservative* Christian tradition.

Second option: the power of God can be defined physically, as control over outcomes at all levels. God is *causality* deified. Worse yet, the God of control also sees to the eternal torment of sinners who defy his control (thus proving to them that his power cannot be eluded in the long run). If this is how God is defined, then humanity is led in a very different spiritual direction. We have a basis for claiming that our own control needs are in effect "sacred." They have cosmic legitimacy. We are encouraged to act out our own fears and hatreds by attacking others—and to call that "the will of God."

That's how Christianity got itself involved in crusades, inquisitions, and horrific religious wars in the 1500s and 1600s.

Fundamentalism and Totalitarianism

There is a second reason why definitions of God matter even to non-believers. In political terms, a controlling God provides theological cover for the human abuse of political and economic power. That's what's going on when fundamentalists claim that their religious liberty is at stake if government blocks their effort to impose what they see as God's rigidly controlling moral demands (for instance, that birth control and gay marriages are forbidden, or that abortion is forbidden even in cases of rape, incest, maternal medical complications, or severely damaged conceptions). The theology of an ultimately controlling God legitimates—indeed, *requires*—human political tyranny at the hands of "believers." When these same believers are biblical literalists immune to arguments based on rigorously established facts, we are in trouble.

I acknowledge that I am making a serious and complex claim about the theological roots of a threat to American democracy and the rule of law. I discuss it from other perspectives in *The Confrontational Wit of Jesus,* chapter 11, and again in *Confronting Religious Violence,* chapter 4. I deconstruct both biblical literalism and papal infallibility in *Confronting Religious Absolutism,* chapters 6–8. In this volume, I will be deconstructing this malignant theological aberration from within the resources of Christian spirituality.

Fundamentalism arises in the same mid- to late-Victorian cultural matrix as secular totalitarian ideologies. That includes Marxism and the conceptual foundation of Nazism. It includes the eugenics movement, derived from Thomas Malthus and Herbert Spenser, misleadingly called "Social Darwinism." It includes blind belief in the "free market" elevated into a god and "competition" regarded as the universal solvent that wipes away all problems everywhere. Each of these "modernist" ideologies is an effort to bring human affairs under strict causal control. (And it's hardly surprising that the control thereby asserted just happens to increase the power, privilege, and wealth of a pre-existing socioeconomic elite.) In the twentieth century, the effort to impose such control caused the death of millions.

We see the same desperate effort to assert top-down control in the "law and order" agenda that the hard Right has pursued since the early 1930s. It has pursued this agenda by creating negative community—community organized around the scapegoating of some target group. (I explain this in more detail in in *Confronting Religious Judgmentalism,* chapters 7–11.) Like social bullies, but on a much larger scale, the negative community defends its own status, privilege, and boundaries by attacking some other group as immoral. They are the damned, not the saved. Like bullied children on a playground, these targeted groups are excluded and attacked in an effort to proclaim the superiority of those claiming to be "morally upright."

Specific targets of hard-Right campaigns have varied over time. In the 1930s it was unionized workers and anyone else who benefited from the New Deal's effort to dial back the rapacious excesses of the Gilded Age "captains of industry." In the 1940s the target was American of Japanese ancestry and, by association, anyone of any Asian ancestry. In due course, the target list included "Leftists" and "liberals," black people, career women, gay people, poor people, progressives, immigrants and refugees, Hispanics, Muslims, environmentalists, experts, scientists, and now moderates. Paul Krugman, the Nobel laureate economist who writes regularly in the *New York Times,* repeatedly describes the same dynamic as it shows up among right-wing economists and politicians talking about economics: they have an orthodoxy that trumps the facts of the matter. Being proved wrong by the data does not slow them down.

Although the target changes, the hard-Right attack stays the same: these people are threats; they are dishonest; they are immoral and sources of moral disorder; they must be stopped at any cost (including shutting down the federal government, defaulting on the national debt, and bringing the legislative process to a complete standstill). These are always *ad hominem* attacks against personal character, not issue-based arguments based on objective facts or peer-reviewed research by scholars at major institutions. They denounce as moral threats to the fabric of the nation anyone in the "reality-based community" who argues on a factual basis for policies serving the common good or protecting our equality before the law. And why? Because the "morality" of the libertarian Right presupposes the ruthless, radically individualist contest of each against all—each of us as miniature gods and goddesses, attempting to impose our will upon one another. Nietzsche: "The weak and the failures shall perish: first principle of our love of man. And they shall be given every assistance."[3]

What *would* Jesus say? Quite possibly something bitterly hilarious. He was a much wittier man than most people realize: centuries of cultural change have obscured his laugh lines. (I do my best to restore some of that brilliant satire in *The Confrontational Wit of Jesus*.)

Given the wealth and public relations talent that have been channeled toward the hard-Right co-opting of Christian tradition, it's hardly surprising that growing numbers of political moderates and progressives now want nothing whatsoever to do with Christianity. The religiously non-affiliated (the "Nones") are now numerous enough to count as a major religious denomination all by themselves. The non-affiliated, the vast majority of whom are ex-Christian, constitute more than 20 percent of the population, and more with each succeeding poll. This group is also disproportionately young. According to the Pew Forum (2015 data), 35 to 37 percent of adults under 40 (born between 1975 and 1995) have distanced themselves in this way.[4]

If that's a rousing generational rejection of hard-Right fundamentalist nonsense, it's great news. But it's also the loss of a major cultural heritage. And that's a disaster. Fundamentalism has co-opted resources of immense cultural value, resources that we need now more than ever in their authentic, pro-social form. This co-opting can be halted, and these pro-social resources reclaimed, by extricating the God of Jesus and the symbolism of Christianity from the clutches of the Religious Right.

---

3. Nietzsche, *The AntiChrist*, section 2.

4. Pew Research Center, "'Nones' on the Rise" and "America's Changing Religious Landscape."

Two Approaches to God-Talk

It's difficult to talk about God in clear, non-dogmatic language that neither presupposes personal belief nor rejects belief as illusory or irrational. But I'm going to try.

Here's the best angle that I see for open-handed framing of the issues at stake: there are two very different approaches to defining God. Let's call these two approaches "theology" and "spirituality." Those labels are a bit imprecise (I'll get back to that momentarily), but they are reasonably workable.

Spirituality defines God as the reality attested to by human spiritual experience. *Theology* defines God as a philosophical concept. At its best, Christian tradition keeps these two categories of definition in some coherent balance, such that each guards against the excesses or liabilities of the other. *At its best,* Christian tradition endeavors to combine the best insights of each approach because, of course, there is an inevitable interplay between spirituality and theology.

Here's why: how we think about God (theology) inevitably influences how we interpret our own spiritual experiences. And our spiritual experiences, if we trust them, shape our theology. In the end, this dynamic interplay explains why so many spiritually sensitive individuals reject Christianity: the controlling God of fundamentalism is wildly at odds with their own intuitive encounters with what they recognize as "holy" or as "sacred."

In each of the other volumes in this series, I have laid out different aspects of the specifically *theological* failures of fundamentalism in its portrait of Christianity as absolutist, judgmental, anti-gay, antiscience, chronically hostile, and so forth. I've kept theological complexity to a bare minimum in those books by focusing relentlessly upon practical issues of immediate political and social concern to any reasonable person. In this volume, I want to talk about spirituality in the same way. I'll do so by looking critically at certain universal human experiences attested to across all cultures and across centuries. These experiences can be and have been explained in many ways. Christianity is one such tradition.

Fundamentalism rejects the sophisticated nuance of Christian spirituality just as it rejects the intellectual complexity of Christian theology. Here's the problem with their account: *they think they know it all.*

And the rest of Christian spiritual and theological tradition humbly and repeatedly admits that we don't know it all. We can't know it all. Not if God is God. Christianity 101 (Intro to God-Talk) flatly insists that the sacred cannot be captured in the nets of analytical intellect no matter how finely woven they may be. We are creating an idol of our own devising when we define God in philosophically absolutist terms as Cosmic Control Incarnate. And we are spinning that idol into a politically dangerous fundamentalism when we use what we have concocted to drape our own fears, hatred, ambitions, and control needs in pseudo-religious legitimacy

Over 4,000 years of Jewish and then Christian tradition, many perfectly sane and ordinary people have experienced God as something real. But we simultaneously experience God as something inexplicable. We experience God as beyond all explaining, despite the volumes of learned commentary and explication offered by systematic theologians—the best of whom also admit that God is beyond anybody's explaining. Christian spirituality among ordinary people is rooted not in the heritage of creeds, catechisms, and church dogmatics but rather in spiritual practices like prayer, meditation, service to others, and the brilliant legacy of religious art, architecture, music, poetry, and storytelling. The arts and the spiritual practices of classic Christian tradition can *evoke* religious experience without explaining it.

The experience of God is like this, or it's something like this: anyone who sees the Grand Canyon realizes simultaneously that all of the Grand Canyon cannot be seen at one time. The experience of God is something like that. It's as if, standing on the rim of that incredible canyon, as if it were clear that *by definition* no one could ever know all of this. Even more to the point, it's also clear that the effort to define—the very effort to "see all of it"— is a literal-minded failure of moral imagination. It's a clueless effort to confine, contain, delimit, and hence *control* that which invites and indeed compels us even while eluding us. God eludes us easily, but not because God is trying to be elusive. The problem is that our expressive resources for articulating such experience are far too small. That's why the arts—including the performance art of liturgy and ritual—have always been so central to Christian spirituality.

All of us know the deep, resonant silence of experiences beyond our ability to articulate. We have all had experiences that we don't have words enough to describe. Furthermore, we all know what it's like to share that silence with someone, to share that sense that *there are no words for this.* For the believer, faith is rooted in some of those moments. Faith is an interpretation of some of those moments. Whether or not you share my interpretation—a commonality I am far too sensible to assume—I *am* confident that at the human level we both know what such moments feel like.

Religion that is rooted in such moments has a profound humility and an instinctive, compassionate deference to others' encounters with the same inexplicable Reality.

My Major Claim

Here's the major claim I'll be making in the pages ahead: Christian spirituality confronts Christian fundamentalism with a simple but profound insight: all God-talk is necessarily and inescapably symbolic. That is, the word *God* functions as a symbol in any statement anyone makes about "God." Explaining what I mean by that—and why it matters—is my goal here. Furthermore, I believe that the properly symbolic God-talk of Christianity requires a mix of humility, compassion, and moral courage. However we acquire such attitudes, they are crucial. Without them, humanity may destroy this planet at some point in the next 500 years.

The first step toward averting that catastrophe is believing that we are not inevitably radical self-seeking "rational actors." We are capable of *not* killing ourselves off. The first step is believing that humanity is deeply and inherently motivated toward collaboration, generosity, courage, compassion, self-sacrifice, and creativity. My faith offers such assurance. What I've been calling "Christian humanist tradition" offers such assurance. With so much at stake, surely these resources within Christianity are worth considering.

Doing so may convince you that it is possible to collaborate with believers and with our communities in what must be a global endeavor enlisting all reasonable people everywhere. We don't need to have identical motives, much less identical belief systems funding our motives. We do need to find one another, and to find ways of working together, despite differences in our belief systems.

One step toward that goal—what I have been trying to offer all along—is a way for outsiders to distinguish between authentic and fraudulent God-talk within Christianity. Here my *Confronting Fundamentalism* project reaches its natural conclusion in a discussion of what can—and what cannot—be said about God. The position I take is as familiar a theological commonplace as anything the tradition has on offer: none of us speak for God. None of us know for sure who God is. We have only our own, partial glimpses. That fact alone confronts and deconstructs the dangerous pretenses of Christian fundamentalism.

The larger, longer Christian tradition flatly insists that God eludes any claim made about God. It says that in texts going back to about 1250 BCE—somewhere on the cusp between the late Bronze Age and the early Iron Age. Given this antiquity, what I will be arguing here is not postmodern. It is a reclaiming of classic theological humility that Christianity lost sight of in its mistaken effort to transform theology into "the queen of sciences."

In the last 500 years, the West has tinkered with a dangerous experiment in supposing that all paradoxes can be resolved into simple fact or else dismissed as insignificant illusion. In doing so, we have cut ourselves off from sources of insight about the human condition, wisdom that now we desperately need. Worse yet, libertarians among us are trying to translate this ancient wisdom into marketing rhetoric for an intransigent, right-wing refusal to collaborate, to examine facts honestly, and to accommodate to multiple honest perspectives on stunningly complicated problems about how best to serve the common good. The hard Right does not care about the common good. They are radically individualist. Competition is the greatest good, in fact the only good—utterly ruthless competition in which the rich would get richer, the middle class would steadily disappear, and the exploited working class would slowly be reduced to Third World desperation.

The God problem—the problem of how to define an elusive God—forces us to grapple with paradox. It forces us onto the ground of the is/not. That's the landscape of literature and the arts. It's the landscape of metaphor and symbolism. It is also the terrain of quantum physics and nuclear weapons. We have to find a way to live on this ground—to live *together* on this ground—if we hope to solve the problems that face us collectively.

—

Let me say it again, one last time: stories and poetry are the most robust, most durable, most nuanced resource we have yet invented for grappling with and successfully transmitting human insight. Implicitly or explicitly, every statement about God is an is/not symbolic claim. In the last analysis, such claims arise from the moral imagination, whose primary speech is metaphor and symbol. Symbolism and metaphor take us beyond the black and white, yes or no, either/or logic whose most dangerous culmination is us versus them.

Us against them scapegoating will culminate in *none of the above* unless we learn, and relearn, how to live in a world constituted by paradox.

Overview of Chapters Ahead

In chapter 2, I will begin as always with a story—in this case, a story not about God but about silence. It's a story about the limits of language. Language has its limits. We can communicate successfully—and understand intuitively—far more than we can explain in words. We can also feel more than we can say.

In chapter 3, *God-Talk 101: The Art That Is Christianity,* I lay out the two essential difficulties framing anything anyone might say about God. First, the human experience of God is both partial and elusive. Second, the human ability to attend to these experiences and to live in the light of these experiences is an artistic practice akin to the practices underlying every other human art. That's a claim I've alluded to repeatedly in every volume of my Confronting Fundamentalism project. Now it comes into the foreground.

What does it mean to reframe the long, complex heritage of Christian God-talk as insight into human experience and wisdom about life choices and their consequences? At least for me, that reframing brought lots of fascinating stuff into focus.

And as it all slid into focus for the very first time, I abruptly understood why religion has been such an enduring aspect of human culture globally and for thousands of years. It's simply not possible to fool that many people for that long. I realized that Christianity is not the elaborate lattice of improbable doctrines that for so many years I so easily ignored as transparently irrelevant to my own life. There's something to it. "God" is not the only way to explain it. I grant that. *But there's something there, however you want to explain it.*

In chapter 4, *The Copernican Turn of Christian Humanism,* I draw the obvious conclusion of my reframing. Christian faith does not orbit around Christian dogmatics and doctrines. It does not orbit around the Bible. It does not orbit around the authority of authoritative intuitional leaders, no matter what claims they make to the contrary. Christian faith orbits around the experience of God.

In chapter 5, *Quantum Theology: The Symbolic Character of God-Talk,* I complicate matters a bit further: any statement about God is necessarily a symbolic claim. Nothing anybody ever says can function as the last word or the absolute truth about God: God cannot be defined or specified, just as we cannot measure simultaneously the momentum and the position of an electron.

In chapter 6, *Theological Weirdness (1): The Symbolic Claim That God Is a Person,* I examine the single strangest Christian belief about God, which is that God is personally present to each of us. That belief rests upon three key features of inward spiritual experience.

In chapter 7, *Poets as Theologians: The Moral Imagination of Christian Humanism,* I focus on an obvious problem with the belief that God is personally present to each of us. It looks like a setup for umpteen kinds of dangerous craziness. Why is Christianity not a morbid mix of unconscious projection and potentially psychotic delusion? Christianity is not lunacy because "God is personally present" is a symbolic claim, not a literal claim. And it follows, then, that *poets,* classically defined as artists of any kind, are the premier theologians. Symbolism is the primary "language" of any of the arts.

In chapter 8, *Moses Debates with a Burning Bush,* I offer a simple close literary reading of a few crucial exchanges in the debate between Moses and his burning bush. These are the exchanges within which God explains to Moses who God is. They are the central biblical text for my claim that anything anyone has ever said about God must be understood as a symbolic statement, not an absolute truth.

In chapter 9, *Moses v. Plato: Translation and the Authority of Theologians,* I take a quick look at why this scene was translated first into Greek and then into Latin in the strongly Platonic ways that it was. They had their reasons. None of these reasons are valid today. We'd be much better off reclaiming the image complex offered by the original Hebrew, which portrays God as both inherently dynamic and essentially beyond human definition. That dynamic indeterminacy accords with our world view far more coherently than a God who is static, radically unchanging, and self-defined as a philosophical proposition.

In chapter 10, *Theological Weirdness (2): The Symbolic Claim That God Is Necessarily Impersonal,* I examine the spiritual traditions, alternatives, and antidotes to literal-minded misunderstandings of the belief that God is something like a "person" who is "personally present" to each of us.

In chapter 11, *What, Then, Can Be Said about God?,* I ask an obvious question: a God about whom we can say nothing definitive might be only theoretically different from a God who does not exist at all. Do I deconstruct Christianity into airy nothingness? Or does Christianity as I understand it in fact provide what Shakespeare called "a local habitation and a name" to centrally important, deeply paradoxical human experiences?

Ultimately, each of us must answer that question in good conscience, with deep respect for the conscientious decisions made by others. But at least this much will be clear: absolutist claims made on behalf of a controlling, violent, and vindictive God are fraudulent claims. They fail to accurately represent the Christian heritage.

And the real heritage, I've discovered, is actually quite interesting. It has profound insights into human experience. These can be explained plainly, without presupposing (much less requiring) belief in what Christians gesture toward with the word *God*.

But first, as promised, that story about what can be said and what cannot be said.

2

1967: What the Cake Said

There was a cake in the break room. It was the very largest size of sheet cake, available only by special order from the bakery department. It was a yellow cake with white frosting, its edges framed in bright blue piping. There was no message on the vast expanse of its creamy white surface: no "Happy Birthday Harold," no "Congratulations Edith," no "Good-Bye and Good Luck Mary Sue."

The cake had first appeared on Monday. It was still there on Tuesday. It was still there Wednesday. On Friday, when I punched in at 3:30 for my usual evening shift as a check-out girl, there it was still. Other cakes disappeared within hours. When I picked up my cash drawer from Heather that Friday, I finally asked her what the cake was for. She hesitated.

"That's Shinichi's Hiroshima Day cake." She glanced at me, then quickly looked away. "He does this every year."

The pain on her face was so clear that I quickly looked away myself. But I felt with equal clarity her quiet, ungrudging respect for this sugar-laden act of remembrance. She understood whatever was being said, wordlessly, year after year, as Shin's cake sat there day after day. After a week it was barely notched around the edges, tiny pieces cut off here and there. It looked if it had been nibbled by mice. The mice of memory, perhaps—mice who scurry inside the walls we build between ourselves and the facts of history.

Heather was my mother's age. Had her husband served in World War II? My father had. All my uncles too, on both sides of the family. What were her war years stories? Was she a war widow?

Our gaze held for a moment. Then she looked away again, out toward the suburban street glazed with heat and dust and the August light. I hoisted my cash drawer onto my hip and walked to my usual check-out lane, the one nearest the door.

On my way to the break room for my mid-evening break, I found Shin restocking shelves in the canned soup aisle. He sat on a milk crate, a open flat of cans balanced on his left knee. I stopped, wanting to say something to him.

This was 1967: I was seventeen and a senior in high school; he was in his mid-twenties. Had he been born in an internment camp? He would have been the right age. That thought didn't cross my mind until just now.

Shinichi looked up at me. His eyes were black, his hair black and straight and almost in his eyes. His face was composed and quietly attentive.

"Your cake," I said. Then words failed me. I stumbled into a silence far deeper than I expected, my heart aching with what I did not know how to say. My father been drafted for the invasion of Japan, an invasion rendered unnecessary by those bombings. Until 1944, Dad had had an occupation deferment as an electrician for the local electric company. He wired transformers in factories. In fact, he had wired the transformers for the atomic bomb lab under Stagg Field at the University of Chicago. But he was drafted in 1944. He made his way home on Christmas Eve of 1945: my oldest sibs were told that Santa had brought him on his sleigh.

That was five years before I was born. If he hadn't made it home, I would not be here. Did I owe my life to the bomb that killed so many in one horrific blaze of light?

I'd seen photographs of what those bombs did. I'd seen photographs of Dresden too, and Pearl Harbor, and photographs of liberated death camps. What later came to be called "the good war" looked to me like a chamber of unspeakable horrors from end to end—and none of the dads ever talked about it. None of them.

Once I made the mistake of asking. Only once. My father told me off in no uncertain terms: never ask a man about his war experience. They need to *forget*. It was one of two or three times I ever saw my dad lose his temper.

Shinichi and I had inherited this world from our parents' generation. So I stood there in the grocery aisle, looking into the depths of the darkest eyes I'd ever seen. Shin returned my level gaze, patient with my loss of words. Then he lowered his eyes and bowed, just a bit, stiffly, from the waist. When our eyes met again, the light in his eyes had changed.

He went back to stacking cans. I went on my way back to the break room. The break room was a cold and desolate space up a narrow flight of metal stairs on the outside wall of the receiving room, near the door to the space where butchers cut up sides of beef. They tracked foul-smelling bloody sawdust onto the concrete floor of the receiving room, which so help me had not been hosed down in decades. The stench carried up to the break room, a space I had come to hate almost as intensely as I hated this job in the first place.

Shinichi's Hiroshima Day cake sat on a foil-covered tray in the middle of a long brown table. The edges of the table were battered aluminum; it bare surface was soft and crumbling, the color and texture of old cardboard. Narrow metal lockers lined the outside wall, opposite the table. Their beige paint was chipping away, revealing an even older layer of green. Half a dozen black metal folding chairs were scattered here and there around the room, some near the lockers, some pulled up to the table.

When I arrived, the room was empty. I was glad for that. I washed my hands slowly, staring at myself in the bathroom mirror until the tap water running over my fingers began to run warm. That startled me out of my reverie. Then I sat down at the table, and cut myself a generous piece of his cake.

How do we signal understanding a cake except by eating a piece? When Shin punched out at the end of his shift, I wanted him to see that someone had done so. I cut myself a good piece, three inches square, not some hesitant nibble.

It took an eternity to eat. Nobody walked in as I did so. I was grateful for that. I didn't want to be misunderstood. Nor did I understand, except for this: of course the cake had nothing to say for itself. It's blank surface attested to what can neither be remembered nor forgotten, what cannot be spoken about and what must be said every August no matter what.

I knew what to *do,* and that was all that mattered. There are times when any of us do what's right, whether or not we have words to explain its rightness. I had no words for it. Neither did Shin, perhaps. Perhaps we had that much in common. That, and the cake, and the heritage of Hiroshima and Nagasaki.

And the proper response, then, was for me to admit that this wordless horror was my history too. I did not forget, I could not forget, no matter how desperately my father and my uncles and my parents' friends and all my friends' fathers and all of their uncles too all needed to forget what they had been through. Shin and I were a new generation. The future belonged to us. Wherever this grim century was taking us, we were on that journey together.

Every August, I notice Hiroshima Day ticking past just as I notice Pearl Harbor Day in December and now, God save us, September 11.

3

God-Talk 101: The Art That Is Christianity

Whatever can be said about God exists in the space between what can be said and what we have no words for. The mute blank surface of Shinichi's cake existed in the same tension: it refused to take sides in an us versus them contest to justify the first-ever use of nuclear weapons. It also refused to forget—or to allow others to forget—what happened on August 6, 1945.

His honesty was courageous. So also it is hazardous to attempt to speak about God while remembering that God is not a topic about which we can speak. Anything anyone might say about God, no matter how persuasive, is ultimately contingent. It is framed by silence, by the ultimate inexpressible. If we forget that fact for a moment then we are wasting our time.

Similarly, there is no ultimate painting after which there is no reason to paint, no ultimate novel after which fiction writers fall silent. The world will always need new music. Grappling with music is like grappling with God: there is and can be no end to this. To engage in God-talk honestly, you must realize that you are joining a *conversation*. Christianity is a conversation sustained over centuries. It is a *tradition*, not a set of controlling absolutes.

Nor is that all. If we could learn how to play the violin by reading books, aspiring violinists would not need violin lessons. But they do. Despite the presence of thousands of books in art history and art theory, aspiring painters still stand in wide circles, each working to paint the same still life under the vigilant eye of a master painter. Writers sign up for writing workshops. Tennis players take tennis lessons. *There are some things you can't learn from books.*

Why is that the case? Why is *theory* not sufficient? If we have musicology and books about playing the violin, why do we still need violin teachers? We need violin teachers, I submit, because mastering the violin is a deeply embodied undertaking. It's not simply verbal or abstractly cerebral. The same is true of any creative process. A *process* is a *practice:* we learn by doing what we cannot learn by theory.

The same is true of the creative practice that is Christianity. It depends upon and is rooted in centuries of religious tradition, just as violin playing depends upon and is rooted in centuries of violin playing and music composed for the violin. But the core practice of *being* a Christian requires an embodied set of skills that arise only with practice: prayer practice, meditation practice, communal worship, and the practice of radical hospitality with people you have not actively and individually chosen as friends.

Christian humanism as I understand it claims forthrightly what has always been widely acknowledged: Christianity is an art. Christianity is an artistic practice akin to songwriting or filmmaking or musical composition and performance. Apprenticeship in the faith begins a long journey into the depth and wholeness of one's own heart, a depth and wholeness wherein God is present to us and we are present to God. Recognizing that presence makes a difference in our lives that anyone ought to be able to see.

Amidst my own "practice of the presence of God," as it is called, I have discovered that my life makes sense.[1] Amidst that presence, I have discovered that my experience is coherent. All of it holds together, even the painful parts. It holds together despite how extraordinarily difficult it remains to articulate that coherence

---

1. The "practice of the Presence of God" goes back to the letter and conversations by that name of Brother Lawrence, a monastery cook in France in the 1600s. It's a wise and charming little book about what today we would call "mindfulness," but in a Christian context. It's available as a free download from the Gutenberg Project, https://www.gutenberg.org/ebooks/5657.

in plain propositional language, without recourse to the poetry or storytelling or one of the other arts media. Amidst that presence, I have become aware of a compassion that flows through me not *from* me. Slowly I've gotten a bit better at getting my self-obsessions out of the way of that flow.

And so I'm convinced that no one can get at what Christianity is getting at about God in the abstract, or from the outside, or without embodied learning by doing. These facts constrain everything anyone might say about God.

I might as well try to explain on the page the smell of bread baking. Or the precise texture of a note played on a violin.

Spiritual Experience

Despite the remarkable difficulty of honest God-talk, we inherit a lot of it. We need to understand that heritage, because it is our essential guide to the artistic practice that is Christianity. We need to grapple with this heritage, just as novelists grapple with the history of the novel or painters grapple with art history.

It seems to me that the artistic heritage for any of the arts has three major components.

1. Classic, definitive performances by past masters. For Christian spirituality, that's the Bible.

2. Studies and commentaries on great performances. For Christian spirituality, that's theology, biblical scholarship, and the vast heritage of teachings called "dogma and doctrine." (Translated into English, *dogma* means "opinion" and *doctrine* means "teaching.")

3. Accounts of the creative process and reflections on how to facilitate or engage the creative process fruitfully. Among writers, for instance, this is the wealth of commentary by writers about the writing process. Novelists talk about novels in dramatically different ways than literary theorists do because novelists are speaking from inside the writing experience. For Christian spirituality, this category includes accounts of spiritual experiences and reflections on how to facilitate or engage

such moments fruitfully.

Let's look at these three categories more closely, one at a time, beginning from the bottom—from the core level human experience of God among perfectly ordinary people.

Accounts of Spiritual Experience

Tradition says that we know about God because God wishes to be known: the reality that is God has been disclosed within human consciousness. But God is not known as objects available to the five exterior senses are known. God is known inwardly and even then only indirectly. As I discovered in my work on Coleridge, there's a lot of tangled argument about how best to name this cognitive alternative to direct sensory knowledge of immediately physical objects. Like Coleridge, I call it imagination (discussed in more detail in *Confronting Religious Absolutism,* chapters 9–12).

In general, there are two sources of spiritual experience. Some are spontaneous or unsought, or what William Wordsworth famously called "spots of time." Accounts of such experiences are remarkably similar. Apparently it's a common human experience. There's a glimpse, more or less brief, of the fact that reality is orderly, breathtakingly beautiful, and benevolent: you are both loved and valuable; so is everyone on earth; life makes sense even though you don't have words for it. (I'll get back to these experiences shortly.)

The other large category of spiritual experience *are* sought. They are the result of sustained, disciplined prayer practice, meditation practice, and so forth. These range from the believer's mundane sense of God's invisible sustaining presence to the extraordinarily vivid experiences described by mystics. (I discuss Christian prayer and meditation practice in *Confronting Religious Denial of Science,* chapters 7-13.)

Spiritual experience is inherently controversial. There are challenges from psychology that what has been experienced is nothing more than the breakthrough of unconscious material. There are challenges from church leaders that individual or mystic experiences are an intolerable threat to institutional stability, good order, received doctrine, and so forth.

The usual reply to either challenge is to insist that individual spiritual experience must of course be cross-examined carefully in a process that tradition calls "discernment." Discernment is obviously crucial: it protects us against craziness and self-deception. It helps us to understand and to examine thoughtfully what we have experienced. Discernment locates us within a community of spiritual explorers, a community that has been sustained over thousands of years.

All of that is invaluable. All of it can also be misused. "Discernment" can be used to silence anyone who dares to doubt the authority of the authorities. Today's "spiritual but not religious" run into that all the time. They are the strict empiricists of God, so to speak, trying to go it alone, trying to make it through without community and without safeguards. Some of them are prophetic voices. Some of them will get lost in the wilderness. It's a risk. It's a risk that more people take during historical periods when institutional religion is both corrupt and self-preoccupied.

And so I bristle every time I hear someone with official church credentials contemptuously dismiss the "spiritual not religious" as narcissists, slackers, and self-indulgent dabblers. Perhaps some of them are. And perhaps some clergy are ignorant, arrogant, predatory, and emotionally abusive. Given this state of affairs, no one is to be condemned nor dismissed for continuing a solitary search for the transcendent. "Sit down and shut up" is a singularly unattractive invitation to join any organization.

But I don't worry much about snide remarks from churchmen about the "spiritual not religious." I am far more concerned that histories of Christian spirituality and anthologies of Christian spirituality systematically ignore the arts, especially the arts of the last 500 years. William James, in his magisterial *Varieties of Religious Experience,* assembles a wonderful variety of anecdotal accounts of spiritual experience. But despite special interest sections within scholarly organization like the American Academy of Religion or the Modern Language Association, there is remarkably little serious theological attention paid to the fully achieved, aesthetically complex artwork that has arisen from spiritual experiences among accomplished artists.

That neglect has developed, I suspect, because taking serious art seriously as insight into God requires a dual competency: both art criticism and historical theology. That's asking a lot. Academia is a forest of silos where genuinely interdisciplinary thinking is often suspect. I saw that repeatedly in the years when I was doing scholarly work on Coleridge: some scholars with theological training knew him as a major theologian; other scholars with literary training knew his literary theory and his poetry. I could count on one hand the few of us who knew both: the literary scholar consensus was that Coleridge's theological interests were a neurotic failure of nerve and an intellectual embarrassment; the religionists couldn't—or didn't—read poetry.

But that's only part of what's going on. The greater part, the deeper part, is that religious dogmatism has a stranglehold on what counts as authentically "religious." To whatever extent this is the case, to that extent the arts are reduced to clichéd "illustrations" of conventional belief. They are not autonomous theology. Thank heavens there are major exceptions to this state of affairs. But these are exceptions that prove the point. I did a major survey once of anthologies of Christian spiritual writing, and I came away in bleak despair at what wasn't there.

Which leads me to the second category of God-talk: studies of great spiritual "performances."

Theology

The second great source of God-talk is theological tradition. "Theology" broadly defined includes 2,000 years of arguments and speculations by critical thinkers interested in God or in Christian tradition. It includes everything from the hyper-academic (then and now) to the utterly popular and everything in between. "Theology" broadly defined also includes the arguments and the historical research of biblical scholars investigating the texts and contexts that we inherit from the ancient world.

"Theology" of these first two varieties is an immense, diverse, contentious conversation. Far more problematic for most people today—inside and outside the church alike—is a third subset of theological speculation: the authoritative dogmas and doctrines that comprise Christian orthodoxy. "Orthodoxy" refers to the broad array of dogmas and doctrines inherited from the ancient world. "Orthodoxy" means "correct opinion," but on the whole orthodoxy does not present itself as *opinion*. It presents itself as the unquestionable believe-or-be-damned *facts* about God. That's quite problematic. As theologian Peter Rollins argues in *How (Not) to Speak of God* (2006), orthodoxy can degenerate into a conceptual idolatry. In that regard, rigid orthodoxy is the mirror twin of biblical literalism. It's a *theological literalism*, perhaps: reading the heritage of orthodoxy in literal-minded ways.

Orthodoxy comes in two large categories. First there are "doctrines," a word that means "teachings." Education is of course an ongoing concern within Christianity, and so if you are watching closely, doctrine does evolve—very slowly—over time and in accordance with cultural change.

The great example of such doctrinal evolution are the catechisms—Christianity's FAQ, suitable for memorizing. As a child, I memorized 367 FAQ from the old "Baltimore Catechism" (1941). (I still have a copy. That's how I know how close I came to memorizing all 499 entries.) We were supposed to memorize the entire catechism prior to Confirmation in fifth or sixth grade. Doing so consumed religion class day after day for a year or so. Some of the opening questions are charming and simple. Others read like instructions from the IRS.

Imagine being handed such a book and told—as a ten-year-old—to memorize it cover to cover for fear of public humiliation by the bishop when he comes. He would select children at random, we were told, demanding that we recite the proper answer to any question he posed. That prospect terrified me. Humiliate my parents in public? That would never do. Under any circumstances—even less terrifying ones—memorizing a catechism is in effect a powerful definition of Christianity itself for any youngster. It's no wonder, then, that in the 1960s and 1970s my generation walked away from Christianity in numbers now being echoed by our children in the millennial generation.

On the whole, each denominations has its own catechism. Periodically new versions are issued—and so when I was in college the new, so-called Dutch Catechism of 1967 showed up on the reading list of a course I was taking.[2] My heart sank at its heft, a full 510 pages. Despite the title, however, it's not written in FAQ format. I didn't memorize any of it, but I did read the whole thing. I was startled by how boldly it differed from the 1941 catechism—and by how engaging how many of its ideas were. Unfortunately, this wasn't the stuff I was hearing preached when I actually went to church.

Doctrine is like that. Doctrine *does* change. But the changes take time to filter down to local congregations. And in each iteration, doctrines generally—and catechisms in particular—pose as *the* answers. *The* answers to *the* questions, Christianity firmly nailed into place. Whatever question you might have, Christianity has its answer book, and these answers cannot themselves be questioned. And so Christianity itself comes across as massively controlling—or at least under the firm control of somebody somewhere. And this somebody does not seem at all open-minded.

That is theologically misleading. To say the least.

Second, there's "dogma," a word that translates "opinion." But not just *any* opinions. Dogmas are the official decrees about doctrines issued by some church authority. Dogmas are the authoritative opinions of men whose opinions matter.

Dogma became dogmatic when it became treason against the king or emperor to question church authority in any regard. As Baylor University historian Philip Jenkins explains in *The Jesus Wars* (2010), centuries of civil wars followed the Roman imperial effort to force a single orthodoxy upon a young, sprawling, and theologically diverse Christianity. Dogmatic rigidity also helped to fuel the devastating Wars of Religion in Europe between 1521 and 1660.[3] Just one thirty-year stretch killed a higher percentage of Europe's population than would later die in World War I and World War II *combined*. Almost twice as many in fact.

---

2. Bishops of the Netherlands, *A New Catechism*.

3. I discuss the great Wars of Religion in *Confronting Religious Absolutism*, chapter 4.

Rigid orthodoxy quickly shattered Protestant Christianity into thousands of different groups, each differing from the others on some exceedingly precise dogmatic issue, each insisting that it has the truth, the whole truth, and nothing but the truth when it comes to God. The more rigidly absolutist church authority is, and the more vehemently "sinners" are threatened with eternal torture in hell, the more appealing it will be for political actors to try to co-opt church authority in support of their own agenda.

In short, serious problems arise when rigid doctrines and dogmas are assembled into an unquestionable orthodoxy. But here's something even more peculiar: this orthodoxy makes less and less sense to anybody as centuries tick by, because our world view is dramatically different from the world view of classical and late-classical antiquity. Orthodoxy offers "correct opinions" regarding abstractly philosophical problems that we no longer have. More dangerously yet, to insist upon the centrality of classic orthodoxy is to insure that Christianity becomes increasingly irrelevant to the urgent moral problem that we *do* face. Christian God-talk today far too often speaks in an elaborate code that fewer and fewer people understand because (a) few people have the philosophical competence required to decode it and (b) more and more people decide at an early age that Christianity makes no sense whatsoever.

I stand squarely within a massive, mainstream tradition in making this complaint. Talking *about* Jesus is much easier than listening to him. It seems to me that if the grand philosophical edifice we inherit from late-classical antiquity is not being used today to pray for enemies, feed the hungry, clothe the naked, shelter the homeless, and welcome the outcast stranger, then it has vanishingly little to do with Jesus himself. It can function as an elaborate intellectual excuse to avoid grappling with Jesus' radical moral vision of human community and human equality.

And that brings me to the third classic source of Christian God-talk: the Bible.

The Bible

As I explain in *Confronting Religious Absolutism,* biblical literalists regard the Bible as God's own direct and immediate self-revelation. Here's how they see things: even though divine self-revelation took place through words written by human authors, Scripture is not subject to human limitations, human history, the influence of human cultural contexts, and so forth. As a result, the text is autonomous and self-interpreting: we don't have to *do* anything in order to understand accurately what it says. God sees to that himself. Somehow. And so the Bible says what it says with a transcultural, transhistorical, God-guaranteed transparency. The Bible is, quite literally, the Word of God. We may not presume to parse it with human analytical tools such as history, linguistics, and cultural studies. Rigorous scholarship is blasphemy, especially when it concludes *Moses didn't write that* or *Jesus never said that* or *the earth and sky as we know them today were not created in a week.*

There are, of course, multiple varieties and gradations of this literalism. Some middle-of-the-road believers admit intellectually that certain limited kinds of biblical scholarship are vitally important. And yet they are emotionally convinced that Scripture has some level of supernatural authority, because for them praying with Scripture has been a major spiritual experience of the presence of God. The depth of their anguish over "questioning what the Bible says" on an issue must never be underestimated.

I don't share that anguish. I've seen it up close; I sympathize. Anybody would. But I don't share that anxiety because, as far as I'm concerned, describing the Bible as a human literary collection in no way diminishes its moral authority and sacred wisdom. As Jesus revealed, it is possible for the divine to be present to us in and through other people. When those other people are artists of any variety, the work that's produced can have a stunning clarity. Christians who panic about regarding Scripture as the work of human hands vastly underestimate the power and the truth value of human storytelling. Biblical scholar Sandra Schneiders explains all this brilliantly in her *Revelatory Texts: Interpreting the New Testament as Sacred Scripture* (1991).

The Bible is the work of human poets and storytellers. It is a breathtaking achievement. Nonetheless, it was composed, edited, redacted, and re-edited to meet the needs to particular communities in particular circumstances. We have to keep that in mind. To fail to do so is to fail to heed the moral imagination and spiritual insight of the human voices who composed this text. Keeping the work in its own proper context makes its limitations less dangerous and its insights all the more stunning.

Or so it seems to me.

Christianity as a Practice

To summarize, then: there are three major categories of God-talk: personal accounts of immediate spiritual experience; theological speculation (including both contemporary, rigorous biblical scholarship and the ancient dogmas and doctrines of Christian orthodoxy); and Scripture itself. In three very different ways, each source provides some necessary insight into Christianity as an artistic practice.

As a practice, Christianity as a way of life. It's not a set of ideas about God. It's a way of navigating the terrain of daily life this week and next. Let me repeat that: *Christianity is a set of vitally embodied practices shaping daily life*, just as playing the flute is a set of practices shaping the daily life of flutists, or sculpture is a set of practices shaping the daily life of sculptors. Or as writers say with some regularity, what it means to "be a writer" is simply showing up at the page on a regular basis. (You want to be a writer? Fine. *Write.* In a disciplined, regular way, *write.*) So also, to be a Christian is to endeavor to see everything through the lens of compassion and the practice of radical hospitality as exemplified by Jesus, recognizing the divine within everyone no matter how distant, how different, or how threatening they might be. *Show up at the page.*

Once again, that's a major assertion, but it's perfectly mainstream within authentic Christianity. I stand by it squarely—and in the next chapter, I'll push it a bit further.

4

The Copernican Turn of Christian Humanism

Let's stop here for a minute, catch our collective breath, and survey where we have gotten thus far: classic tradition says that there are three sources of knowledge about God: direct, individual spiritual experience; theology; and the Bible. So far, so good.

But there's a catch. In practical political terms, these three sources are far from equal. Spiritual experience has commonly been subordinated to theology and to Scripture, both of which have been kept firmly under the interpretive control of institutional authority. Which is to say: one way or another, the church speaks for God.

In its sharply authoritarian turn since the mid-1800s, Roman Catholic tradition is now forthright about this state of affairs: to be legitimate, spiritual experience must be consistent with the official teachings of the Magisterium. As I explained a few minutes ago, Protestant tradition, although originally quite individualist, quickly fell into intense and remarkably violent conflicts over very abstruse theological distinctions. As a result, Protestants today are *more* likely to defer to the authority of Protestant church teachings than Catholics are to defer to the Catholic church.[1]

And so my claim holds: to all extent and purposes, among Catholics and Protestants alike, *the church speaks for God and about*

1. Pew Research Center, "U.S. Religious Landscape Survey: Religious Practices and Beliefs."

God. Each church does so somewhat differently, by reference to its own internal array of dogmatic claims, which are the lenses through which they read Scripture. In their own favorite translations, of course. And the people in the pews pay more or less attention to what the authorities attest. I'm not the only person out here in the pews asking restive questions. Not by a long shot.

Christian humanist tradition as I understand it centers itself instead upon the human experience of God. Let me say that again: *God.* God as known in the human heart, in particular inward human experiences by particular people. *Spirituality,* in short.

Christian humanism orbits around God, not around the pronouncements of councils and committees. It does not orbit around the long conversation, part scholarship and part politics, documented in our vast heritage of creeds, catechisms, dogmas, doctrines, and confessions of faith issued by institutions. No. It does not.

Neither is Christian humanism centered on Scripture. The Bible is invaluable, but the Bible is not God. Only God is God.

And God is at the center of Christian humanism. More precisely, Christian humanism as I understand it orbits around a single reality: God exists and God wishes to be known. God seeks relationship with us. Our efforts to write about our response to God's initiative and our experiences of God's initiatives take various textual forms: the poetry and narratives of Scripture; philosophical statements ancient and new; and the narrative, poetic, and artistic accounts arising from individual spiritual experience. Some of these texts are older, and they rightly earn the prestige of their antiquity. Some are newer, and they rightly earn our esteem by speaking to us in a language and within cultural contexts that make the experience of God understandable in our own day.

But none of these texts are God. Only God is God. And the God who defined himself as one who will be what he will be is not captured in or confined by any work of human hands. All of these texts—all of them, including the Bible—are works of human hands. They are the written voices of other people. Some of these writers were or are geniuses—I grant that. I am profoundly grateful for them. But even a genius is a person living at a particular moment in a particular place.

Within this Copernican turn, both Scripture and theology change character. They are redefined as fallible human accounts of fallible, inevitably partial human spiritual experience—as things people wrote down in response to encounters with *what they took to be God.*

Scripture and theology remain in place after this Copernican turn, just as the Ptolemaic observations and data sets of Tycho Brahe remained in place after the Copernican turn in astrophysics, and just as the finding of classical physics remained in place after the development of quantum physics. Nonetheless, we see Brahe's data differently now. It now attests to a different reality, to a new understanding of the stars overhead at night. We interrogate this data differently. We ask new questions.

So also we see both theology and Scripture very differently after the Copernican turn in Christianity. Within that changed perspective, new questions emerge. New questions emerge because we allow dogma, Scripture, and individual experience variously to interpret and interrogate one another. Amidst that interplay, certain deeply problematic claims (especially regarding the violence of God—e.g., the genocide of Canaanites, the prospect of eternal torture in hell) begin to be reframed as salutary warnings against our human capacity to project upon God. This vast and at times contentious conversation could not be more distinctively Jewish if it tried.

There is a story told that one day God appeared to two rabbis who had spent their lives arguing about the meaning of a single text.

"Let me tell you what I meant," God says.

"Who are you to tell us!" the rabbis protest in unison. It was the first time they ever agreed on anything.

And the story is told because it is in struggling with our experience of God that we encounter God most clearly—that infuriating, elusive, nameless character who chuckles like the Cheshire Cat in his tree. And then vanishes.

The center of Christian humanism—the elusive, fiery center of it all—remains God's creative spirit interacting disruptively with our creative spirits. We encounter that center through the moral imagination or not at all. The question then—the really difficult question—remains in place. The question stands at the center of everything that makes Christianity culturally significant: *Who is God? What is God? What do we mean when we use that word?*

There are no absolute answers. That's my point. But there are indeed answers.

5

Quantum Theology:
The Symbolic Character of God-Talk

Because we inherit the Bible, we inherit a thousand-year-long literary tradition of *personifying* God as a character. In many of these stories, God is portrayed as a humanlike entity who says things, does things, sends messengers, shows up in dreams, rescues people, destroys people, gets angry, repents of his wrath, cares about the downtrodden, and so forth. The scriptural character THE LORD God is by far the most brilliantly realized character in all of classical literature. "God," as tradition has come to call him, is by any measure the most influential literary character in all of Western tradition.

The character "God" portrayed in the Bible bears no resemblance whatsoever to the essentially Greek philosophical concepts that were later added to his job description, layered atop his dramatic narrative personality. And that was a setup for trouble.

Roughly speaking (sweeping generalization alert), here's what happened. In classical antiquity in the first few centuries after Jesus, THE LORD God of Scripture was redefined theologically. Atop his narrative identity, God now personified Neoplatonic philosophical concepts such as *causality* or *existence* or *the Good*, the *summum bonum*. More than a thousand years later, in the 1700s, Deism de-personified this complexly layered personification, leaving us with God the Abstract Concept (causality, control, morality). And then philosophers pointed out that abstract ideas do not refer to independently existing realities. (There is no *Tree*. Trees we have. Millions of them. But *Tree*? *Tree* does not exist. It's only an abstract generalization from our experience of trees.) Abstract concepts lacking an anchor in sensory experience became suspect. They're artifacts—nothing but wordplay. In 1739, David Hume used an argument like this to discredit both "causality" and academic theology—a revolutionary argument.

Such developments downsized God out of his previous role in the West's world view. He was rendered obsolete and unnecessary. As a result, the whole doctrinal-dogmatic orthodox shebang appeared to collapse because it had no anchor in direct sensory observation of immediate physical realities. And the remarkable confidence with which Christianity continued to talk about "God" began to look like a mix of blazing arrogance and dangerous irrationality.

Here's the problem as I see it. Worship services can seem blithely to portray God as a more or less humanlike character out there somewhere. Like any other superhero, he has powers that far surpass our own. *Anthropomorphism*, anthropologists call it: imagining the gods as people with superpowers. This is God the Father Almighty, that toga-clad character with the flowing beard. This is also the God whose death was proclaimed in the 1880s. It doesn't demand a degree in philosophy to stand in the back of a church wondering *what are these people talking about?*

It's as if nobody told the churches that God the Abstract Concept has been deconstructed as a merely verbal artifact left over from the obsolete world view of medieval Scholasticism or ancient-world Neoplatonism. We no longer need propositions like "Ground of Being" or "Uncaused Cause." Christianity can seem to be a cultural zombie—neither dead nor alive but a serious threat to everyone else. And especially so, needless to say, when Christianity is reduced to a public relations strategy by the hard Right in its effort to garner support for libertarian policies by appealing to dark "nativist" and racist strands in American culture.

No wonder so many reasonable, morally sensitive people have walked away. Who can blame them?

Personification and Metaphor

Here's my comeback to all of these developments: personification is not the same thing as anthropomorphism. Personification is a variety of metaphor. The metaphoric personification of God permeates Scripture. It permeates theological tradition. You will hear it in church every Sunday. *No matter what it sounds like at times,* any personification of "God" is at heart a metaphor: it is calling something by the name of something else. Christianity that loses sight of its own metaphors *as metaphors* is descending into literal-minded fundamentalism.

God—what we mean to name by that noun—is in some ways *like* a person just as delight is in some ways *like* champagne or despair is in some ways *like* an endless night. But for the metaphor to succeed in communicating what it is trying to communicate, we must simultaneously remember that joy is not champagne, despair is not darkness, and God is not a person or a person-like entity "out there someplace." We must be able to hold in mind the is/not character of the metaphor if we are to understand the point of the comparison.

Let's stop here for a moment to stare at that fact. Ordinary, commonsense Aristotelian logic would insist that either God is a person or God is *not* a person: we can't have it both ways. Trying to have it both ways is flat-out contradictory. It's a mistake. Or it's sleazy, like the fine print in contracts meant to deceive the consumer.

That's why, in mid-1600s, the very first funded research project of the newly commissioned Royal Academy for the Advancement of Science was to engage John Wilkins to invent a language in which metaphor would be impossible. Metaphors were lies, it was thought, and science must avoid them at all costs. But today's cognitive linguists—people like George Lakoff and Mark Johnson—have reconfirmed what John Wilkins explained to the Royal

Academy in his final report of 1668: metaphor inescapably permeates all language.[1]

Metaphor in all of its varieties is as essential a conceptual
tool as quantum mathematics. Almost a century now of quantum
physics has demonstrated that what "common sense" would call
impossible logical contradictions are nonetheless constituent of
reality at the subatomic level. Metaphor, I'd argue (and I'm speaking
metaphorically here myself), is our much older conceptual tool for
grappling with equally acute contradictions in our understanding
of reality at the spiritual level. Just as quantum physics is prerequisite for computer chips, and computers have had a massive cultural
impact, so also a proper understanding of spiritual reality is prerequisite for Christianity, and Christianity has had an equally massive
cultural impact for thousands of years.

In short: we can only grapple with important aspects of human
spiritual experience and make full use of our critical intelligence if
we have the conceptual tools—like metaphor and symbolism—that
allow us to grapple with what seems to "common sense" to be impossible logical contradictions. Metaphor and symbolism are human
intellectual achievements no less central than the mathematical
skills of quantum physics. As a cognitive skills, these abilities are
an antidote to literal-minded fundamentalism and to the politics of
stalemate and grandstanding that hard-Right fundamentalism has
generated.

Metaphor and the "Personhood" of God

The "personhood" of God is a premier instance of a radically
metaphorical claim. From some perspectives, it is vitally true. From
other, equally valid perspectives, it is completely false. I'll explain
why shortly. But first I want to talk a little bit more about metaphor.

God is not a metaphor. Let me be clear about that. Metaphors
permeate God-talk as people grapple with the difficulty of explaining their experience of God, but God is not a metaphor. God is a

---

1. The bibliography at the back provides details of several books by Lakoff and Johnson. For more detail on John Wilkins, see my essay, "Coleridge's
Theory of Language," also in the bibliography.

complex reality that can be discussed or defined only metaphorically. Or symbolically. But what does "defined symbolically" mean? Let me explain.[2]

Metaphor has been defined since the days of Aristotle as calling Thing One by the name of Thing Two: the *Harris tweed* cat, the *howling* wind, feeling *down in the dumps,* or *plowing* through a difficult book. Thing One, the immediate thing we are trying to describe, is the cat, the wind, the mood, the book. Thing Two, the secondary or "borrowed" thing, is Harris tweed, wolves, landfills, and agricultural plows in the days before tractors, when plowing demanded extraordinary upper body strength. To understand what each of these metaphors is trying to tell us, we must be able to keep in mind *simultaneously* that the cat is/not Harris tweed, that the wind is/not a wolf, and that depression is/not living in a garbage dump, and so forth. We must have the imaginative prowess necessary to conceptualize paradox and to manipulate paradoxes in a precise, delicate way. We have to be able to think *by analogy* without getting the lines of the analogy so tangled that we fall flat on our faces. (To speak *by analogy* to walking more than one dog at once.)

Symbol is a special case of metaphor because in a symbol, all we can get our hands on is Thing Two, the borrowed something. Symbols borrow from something known in order to illuminate an aspect of something unknowable directly. This Unknowable something is by definition elusive. It is beyond the reach of ordinary rational understanding and direct sensory perception. It is knowable only partially and only by indirection—only by analogy to something that we *do* know and we *can* get our hands on.

Let me say that again. A symbol uses the Known to evoke the Unknowable that hovers just outside our range of vision. Symbols call into consciousness that which exists at the liminal edge between conscious and unconscious, which is to say on the border between body and mind.

The object of a symbol—the Unknowable Thing One—is best understood as a domain of human experience to which we have limited conscious access. An example might help here. As I explained

2. I discuss symbolism at much greater length in *Confronting Religious Absolutism,* chapters 9–12. But we need a quick summary here.

in *Confronting Absolutism,* chapter 11 (one of several examples I offer there), the great white shark in the movie *Jaws* is a symbol. The shark is a Thing Two that evokes an enormous, elusively complex Thing One. Included in this "Thing One" domain are the following: fear, anger, violence, guilt, loss, the unconscious, the weight of history, the burden of having technology such as the atomic bomb, the fragility of civilization, the nature of a man's obligation to protect his community, and so forth. The symbol that is the shark, as situated within the film, organizes that whole list of elements into a specific and unique configuration.

And yet despite how specific this configuration is to that film, we recognize in our own lives the reality that the shark symbolizes. Coleridge explains that our heads snap up—our hearts leap up—when we encounter an authentic symbol, just as a man, sitting in a bar in a foreign country, might pivot in an instant at the sound of his own native language. *The lonely guy in a bar hearing his own language for the first time in years*—at the end of the day, that's one of the best definitions of "symbol" out there.

It's a metaphor. *It's an analogy.* And it communicates brilliantly.

An effective symbol speaks to what Alexander Pope described as "what 'oft was thought, but ne'er so well expressed." *Been there, seen that* we want to say, and yet we haven't, not in the same way, not with the same clarity. That's why we reread great novels, rescreen great films, memorize favorite poems: each time we encounter the symbolic reality, we are that lonely guy in a bar all over again, our heads snapping up because we have heard a voice speaking the language of our own deepest, most elusive, visceral reality.

And that's not all. It's not just that symbols refer to the Unknowable or the barely knowable by means of the Known. There is a further truth here, which is that the Unknowable is otherwise available to consciousness only as a contradiction. There is contradiction in any metaphor, of course: the wind is not a wolf; delight is not champagne; and so forth. But symbolism, as a rich and potent category of metaphor, takes that contradictoriness to exponential levels.

Consider this, for instance: in the film *Jaws,* the hapless sheriff who finally does kill the shark is the one guy among three on the boat who knows nothing about sharks. Unlike the other two men, he also knows nothing about the sea. He can't even swim. He is terrified of the water and intensely uncomfortable on the boat, where the other two men feel right at home.

Yet, paradoxically, he is the one who kills the shark. He does so only by remembering his own dangerous naïveté about the hazards of oxygen tanks. What does this whole array of contradictions regarding the protagonist sheriff tell us about the all the issues I listed earlier? What does it mean that he is a *sheriff*, given our narrative and filmic experience with "sheriffs" as characters? What does it mean that oxygen tanks in question are for humans diving into the underwater domain of the fish?

And then, of course, there's the most potent contradiction of all: the shark must be a real shark in order to symbolize a configuration of ideas that have very little to do with *carcharodon carcharias* itself. The great white shark of the film is/not simply a shark. It must be a fish and yet something other than a fish—both, simultaneously—in order for the symbolism of the film to resonate as it does to our own deepest fears. In order to speak to us as that lonely figure in a bar.

What do all these contradictions tell us about the larger, barely accessible Thing One Unknown that the shark symbolizes? What does it tell us about how we might ourselves engage with that Unknown when, like the shark, it intrudes upon our daily lives?

Lots. What, exactly? *Watch the movie.* The movie itself will lead you to a fuller experience of that which the shark symbolizes than anything anyone can possibly say. That's why it was necessary to make the movie: these particular insights are not fully accessible in any other way than by watching the movie. And the movie, let me repeat, although very lovely in its own way, offers an extraordinarily simple instance of symbolism. But even simple, somewhat campy symbols are nonetheless very sophisticated conceptual tools.

God-talk, on the other hand, deploys symbolism in some of the most complex, sophisticated ways that I have ever encountered. The inescapably symbolic character of legitimate God-talk attempts to illuminate something about the human encounter with the sacred. And at the core of that human encounter is an immense contradiction: God cannot be known in any direct and complete way. We experience *something*, that's for sure. But we experience it as a glimpse of something that we realize is both inescapably beyond our ken and simultaneously the most powerfully *real* reality we have ever encountered.

⬥

What exactly the human figures in the Bible encounter when they encounter the character named "THE LORD God" cannot be extricated from the stories themselves, tidied up, dehydrated, sliced thinly, and served up as a pure conceptual abstraction on some philosophical platter. Neither can the encounter with the shark in *Jaws*. Why not? Because the meaning and the reality to which even a very simple symbol attests has no simple paraphrasable content. Nonetheless, the reality of "God" is the single greatest symbolic claim made by the human moral imagination.

In the remaining chapters of this book, I will try to walk you through the essential contradictions involved in that claim. My goal in doing so is to arrive, in the end, at something that can be said—plainly and directly—about what it means to me to be a Christian humanist.

6

Theological Weirdness (1): The Symbolic Claim that God Is a Person

When theologians talk about the "personhood" of God, they are speaking *by analogy*: that's how any metaphor works, and especially the subset of metaphor called "symbolism." *From the human side,* then, a relationship with God is something *like* a relationship with a person. "Person" is the familiar, known reality by which theology seeks symbolically to illuminate the sacred Unknowable.

But "personal" is not a literal-factual descriptor of God. It is a symbolic statement: we experience relationship with God as something *like* a personal relationship. That is, God can be at times "personally present" to us: we can have an experience of God that we can only explain *by analogy to* our experience of the presence of another person. But this "personal" claim is a multidimensional symbolic complex. It functions on at least three different levels or dimensions. Each of these dimensions can be construed as an answer to a pointed question: *in what way* does the presence of God or a relationship with God resemble our experiences of another person?

I have three answers to that question. Let's look at them one at a time.

The Impossibly Convincing Glimpse

The first reason is fairly obvious: loving-kindness, empathy, understanding, and compassion are interpersonal realities. They are qualities of *relationships*. One of the most basic religious experiences is a glimpse—perhaps only a momentary, once-in-a-lifetime glimpse—of love and compassion as overwhelming cosmic realities.

One of my favorite literary accounts of this experience is a poem by Marie Howe.[1] The speaker of the poem "sees" something, we are told; it "hails" her. As we will realize soon enough, she is not "seeing" something unequivocally physical, like a person standing in front of her. The experience she goes on to recount is far more elusive and inward than meeting a friend on the street.

What has hailed her? What *is* this? That's the core question posed by innumerable accounts of such experiences: *what is this?* Howe doesn't offer a simple answer. She doesn't *have* a simple answer. The most compelling and vivid accounts of such experiences never have simple answers. Quantum theology argues that there are no simple answers.

What Howe does have, what the poem does offer us, is a vivid portrait of an enigmatic experience. She offers no metaphysical explanation. She just says—the lyric voice always says—*this is what happened. Let me tell you what happened to me.*

> Even if I don't see it again.—nor ever feel it
> I know it is—and that if once it hailed me
> it ever does—
>
> and so it is myself I want to turn in that direction
> not as towards a place, but it was a tilting
> within myself,
>
> as one turns a mirror to flash the light to where

1. This poem is reprinted in Housden, *Dancing with Joy*, 146.

it isn't.—I was blinded like that—and swam
in what shone at me

only able to endure it by being no one and so
specifically myself I thought I'd die
from being loved like that.

Note the apparent failure of grammatical parallelism in line 5. The phrase "not as towards a place" leaves us expecting "but as towards a [something]." That expectation is momentarily frustrated. A clause intervenes ("but it was a tilting/ within myself") before the parallel construction is completed: "not as toward a place, but . . . as one turns a mirror to flash the light".

Where is that mirror? It is within her. It is something "tilting" (or turning) within her that catches the light. Having had this experience once, she now desires to repeat it, to turn not externally but internally so as "to flash the light to where/ it isn't"—that is, into her eyes and all around her. The speaker of the poem (its "narrator") knows that she might not be able to tilt the mirror again to exactly the same angle, but she's convinced that *if she could* then the experience would repeat: "if once it hailed me/ it ever does—". The experience would repeat because something like "light" is always there.

What is this light? We are not told. But we're told it is blinding. We're told that it is as if something she can swim in. These are logically incompatible physical definitions of the light, but Howe is not doing physics. She is deliberately playing one image off the other in order to recreate for us in physical terms the interior experience of "being loved like that"—being loved with a love that both annihilates her sense of self and radically affirms it.

For better or for worse, ancient Hebrew scriptural-literary tradition has always personified the reality that the speaker of this poem has encountered. The psychological basis of this scriptural-literary personification is obvious: narrative logic requires that for such a loving relationship to be possible, the scene must include two characters *who are capable of loving and cherishing one another.* In these strange, momentary glimpses, I'm one of those characters. Who is the other?

That's a glimpse of God, Christians say of such experiences. *That's an encounter with the divine.* That is, God is personally present to each of us. There exists that which we call "God," and—so to speak—this is "how God feels" about us. That's the primal experience of God's personal presence.

It may be a very muted perception, like a low, soft hum of a distant interstate or like hands softly cupping us as we might hold a small and newly hatched bird. *Something like* any of that: a remote, visceral-emotional sensation almost entirely beyond the reach of consciousness. Or it might be something vivid and sharp, a momentary insight like the flash of a camera going off in our eyes, or like landscape suddenly suffused with a light that offers meaning, not simply photons.

A CTA Train in August

Written accounts of these dramatic experiences often situate them in scenes of great natural beauty. But I knew a man who had such a moment riding a Chicago Transit Authority train. He was a sophisticated, successful "character" actor, a fairly wealthy man, quick-witted and skeptical and uncommonly comfortable with strong women. His wife and I were friends.

One day we were talking about home remodeling—the two of them had just been through that—when he told me a story about an experience on the CTA elevated train running from Evanston south into the city.

The train was rattling and swaying along on elevated tracks that had not been rehabbed in decades—a sway so acute in those days that a susceptible person might have become seasick. The train was crowded. The air conditioner was broken and the windows did not open. The August sun was merciless. It was, he said, like being trapped in a parked car with dozens of sweaty strangers.

As the train approached the center city and curved to go underground, its wheels screeching in metallic protest, suddenly it was, he said, as if each person on that swaying train shimmered not with misery but with God's overwhelming love. Something like a light illumined each of them. In that light, it was as if he too could see the extraordinary beauty of each human soul. And he too loved them.

It was real, he said. It was unreal. He was convinced. He could not believe he was convinced. This was not a God who damned anybody to hell. This was a God seeking to rescue us from the hell that is already here. This was not the God he had heard about in church growing up. He had no idea what to do with this experience, which is why he was telling me about it. He wasn't hallucinating. He was hot, yes, but only sweaty, not dizzy or faint. He was fully *there*. And, as quickly as it had come on, the perception faded away.

After telling me all this he sat there, silent, watching me intently. I waited, equally silent, wondering if he would have anything further to say. His handsome face, the expressive face of an actor, was almost visibly crosshatched by the sheer inexplicability of what had so undeniably happened to him. What could I do but nod, wordlessly? Yes, it seems crazy. No, it's not crazy at all. Both literary and spiritual traditions are replete with such accounts.

The Human Experience at Stake Here

This experience of love or compassion as cosmic realities is not a specifically *Christian* experience. It is a human experience. Different religious and cultural traditions account for such moments in different ways. Christianity is simply one way, one conceptual language—one language among many true and valuable languages—for sharing such experiences and grappling with them both wisely and humanely.

The teachings of Christian spirituality offers ample resources for thinking critically about what happened to him—what has happened to many of us, more or less immediately, more or less vividly, more or less consciously. It is a sense that something profoundly loving is *personally* present to us, present to us as the richly individual quirky characters that we are. As Carol Lee Flinders—a literary medievalist and Buddhist—says in her discussion of the medieval mystic Mechthild of Magdeburg, "God is everywhere and surely, therefore, impersonal; and yet in relation to the individual soul, God is entirely intimate and surely, therefore, personal. . . .

God is there, Mechthild insists, for every one of us, not in a general, impersonal sense, but *there*—so exquisitely right for you it's as if you'd made him up."[2] Her phrase "so exquisitely right for you it's as if you'd made him up" resonates with Howe's final lines, "only able to endure it by being no one and so/ specifically myself I thought I'd die/ from being loved like that."

Mechthild's incredulity was my experience and hence my concern in the aftermath of such moments in my own life. Am I making this up? *Something is "there" for me*—but could it possibly be real? That was the essential conflict riveting my actor friend: it is impossible to doubt the reality of what has been experienced and yet equally difficult to accept that such things are possible.

If such a moment has never erupted in your life, I cannot begin to explain to you how inexplicably, impossibly real it feels. I can only admit, with the deep humility of my own incredulity, that from the outside such experiences do sound crazy.

I'll get back to that issue shortly.

Moral Obligation

This bring me to my second answer to the question of *in what way* relationship with God resembles relationships among people: the relationship is mutually obligating.

Let me explain. Healthy interpersonal relationships are much more complex than "I love you, you love me." On its own, unqualified, that's pure sentimentality. It's nothing more than a theme song suitable for a cartoon character. Toddlers at the time were enchanted by it. Parents at the time gritted their teeth. If you don't know the song nor the cartoon character, count yourself blessed.

As all of us already know, healthy relationships involve mutual obligations and responsibilities. There are reciprocal duties. To say, as theological tradition certainly does, that "God is personally present to us" is also to say that spiritual experience entails more than momentary glimpses of great love. From that love flows equally powerful experiences of moral obligation: one is called to

2. Flinders, *Enduring Grace,* 44.

responsibility for the common good. I think it was evangelical pastor Tony Campolo who said that faith ought to burn calories: we are not called to a vaguely benign love of everybody. That too is mere sentimentality.

Christian spiritual teachings, especially the traditional practice called "discernment," offer remarkably rigorous methods for thinking through what this obligation might mean in one's own life. I summarize that discernment practice in *Confronting Religious Judgmentalism,* chapter 12, and in the last two chapters of my book, *Selling Ourselves Short* (2003). The power of such moments does not constitute an excuse for giving way to some immediate psychological compulsion. Neither does vivid spiritual experience provide an excuse for ignoring substantive argument and data and fact-based analysis. In a very hard-nosed way, spiritual tradition insists that compulsion and the refusal to listen to contrary arguments constitute unequivocal evidence that a person is self-deceived.

Dynamic Change

And this brings me to the third answer to the question *in what way* does relationship with God resemble relationships among people: the relationship is acutely dynamic. Change is central to any healthy interpersonal relationship. In any human relationship, the people involved grow and change through the vicissitudes of coping with the challenges of honest and mutual reciprocity. In that process, as I explained in my book *For Fidelity* (1998), love itself deepens beyond the narcissism of *I love you because you love me.*

In a human relationship, we learn over time to love the other *as other,* and not simply because they love us. It is a long and challenging process. If the relationship is a healthy one, the people involved change for the better, becoming more mature, more resilient, more forgiving, and so forth. After all, rigidity is not taken as a sign of emotional health among human beings.

If God is "personally present" in God's relationship to humanity, then our experience of God, our knowledge of God, will also change and deepen over time. There is far more to the divine than our individual experiences of God's personal and sustaining presence. *God* may not be objectively changing—God is unknowable in any objective way—but our *experience* of God necessarily and inevitably changes, partly as a result of *our* individual change, and partly as a result of cultural change.

Among these cultural changes, for instance, has been an evolving attitude toward slavery and the moral significance of individual human rights. Contemporary attitudes toward such things would have been unimaginable in the ancient world. And yet our attitudes arose over centuries, in documentable ways, from moral reflection on the venerable Jewish teaching that we are all, poetically speaking, made in the image of God and commanded to be generous to strangers. If we are all equally beloved as "children of God," then all of us have "sibling" obligations to one another. The social and political consequences of that biblical teaching have been massive. Nonviolence or non-harming is a morally difficult teaching whose full implications we still struggle to understand, much less to implement.

The dynamic character of our experience of God is inevitable. To whatever extent that our identities—our sense of self—are culturally contexted, to that same extent the culture in which we find ourselves will shape every important relationship we ever have. That includes our relationship with what we take to be God, and what we understand to be the moral obligations consequent upon that relationship.

Christian humanism differs sharply from Christian fundamentalism on this point. Fundamentalists already know—they know for a fact and in great detail—exactly what God demands on any of the difficult questions facing our society today. God wants what they want, and so they need not attend to the ideas, perceptions, arguments, and evidence presented by anyone else. God is not with anyone else. God is only with them.

But the God who is proclaimed by Christian tradition is with *all of us*. Equally. Believers and nonbelievers alike, Buddhists and Baha'i no less than Baptists and Ukrainian Orthodox. That is why we are called to love one another and—a no less difficult challenge—to listen to one another openly and humbly.

The whole point of Jesus, theologically speaking, is demonstrating that God is also present to us in and as *other people*. As theologian Terry Nelson-Johnson explains, Jesus incarnated God transparently or wholeheartedly, and so Jesus became personally identified with this incarnational potential.[3] But all of us, each of us, incarnate or embody God to the extent that we make ourselves translucent to the divine light that shines within every human being, no matter how badly obscured at times.

❧

To summarize, then: there are three answers to the crucial question, "in what way is our experience of God *metaphorically similar* to our experience of one another?"

First, we experience loving supportive presence of a kind that feels very much like what our closest friends and family provide.

Second, as in our human relationships, our relationship to this supportive presence entails or comes to entail moral obligation: the God who loves us so intensely loves everyone else in exactly the same way, and that ought to constrain our behavior in signal regards.

Finally, our sense of our own experience of divine presence is as culturally constructed as our sense of what it means to be a friend, or a parent, or a sibling, or a responsible member of the human community. Those change. Over centuries, those have changed dramatically. So also there has been change in what it means to us to be in relationship with a God who is personally present to us and within us—and also to and within everyone else. There have been changes in our sense of moral obligation to other people.

Despite the psychological intimacy of our experience of God's personal presence, in Christian humanist tradition these experiences always remain appropriately constrained by a single key teaching: we do not know God *directly*. Because the experience of God's personal presence can be psychologically quite vivid, some believers might feel as if they do know God "face-to-face," so to

---

3. Nelson-Johnson is Resident Theologian Presenter at Old St. Patrick's Church in Chicago. I heard him say this in a talk one evening.

speak. That is a misperception. In the poetic language of Scripture, no one looks upon the face of God and lives.

For thousands of years, the Jews have been both elaborately careful and conceptually elegant on this issue: nothing said about God—in Scripture, from a pulpit, from a broadcast studio—can ever be taken *literally* or as some absolutely true claim about God. We are not even to speak the name of God aloud, Jews insist. That is the wisdom Christians inherit—and there is no responsible understanding of the Gospels whereby to circumvent this radical theological humility.[4] *We have no direct knowledge of God, and we must never speak as if we do.*

That teaching has enormous implications. Let's take a look at those next.

---

4. For more on the limits of what we can legitimately say about Scripture, see *Confronting Religious Absolutism,* chapter 7, "Reading Ancient Texts Accurately" and *The Confrontational Wit of Jesus,* chapter 4, "Teaching in Parables: Metaphor, Imagination, and Satire."

7

Poets as Theologians: The Moral Imagination of Christian Humanist Tradition

There's an obvious argument against the possibility that God is personally present to us. In its simplest form, it goes like this: there are seven billion people on earth, which is one insignificant planet among an uncountable multitude of planets where life might exist. Over thousands of years in which our species has existed, countless more of us have been born and died. Have each of these individuals been individually known and loved? To many good and morally sensitive people, the idea borders upon lunacy. If it's not frankly delusional, it is so terribly naive that no intelligent person would consider the claim for an instant.

I have despaired at times—I have despaired repeatedly—that few of my fellow Christians seem to understand the solid grounds for this disparaging incredulity. Their personal relationship with God is so central to their identity, and they are so deeply embedded socially in a community where the reality of a personal God is everywhere assumed, that they cannot fathom how ridiculous their beliefs look to nonbelievers.

The problem, of course, is many people—believers and nonbelievers alike—fail to understand that the statements "God is a person" or "we have a personal relationship with God" are both symbolic claims. Such claims are an effort to illuminate something we cannot otherwise apprehend by something we can. Talk about the "personhood" of God are an effort to flash some light onto what is otherwise a stunningly inexplicable experience.

Are we nuts? Should we call a psychiatrist? Should we shrug and write off such experiences as transparently meaningless? These are honest questions. For thousands of years, spiritual masters have honestly engaged these skeptical challenges. At the same time that the tradition encourages believers to recognize the personal presence of God, it has always surrounded that teaching with sophisticated cautions and safeguards against what today we would call *projection* or *unconscious contents* or *self-deception* or *narcissistic self-absorption*. Evelyn Underhill's great compendium *Mysticism* (1911) is replete with stern cautions and probing doubts. The primary safeguard, theologically speaking, is that no one sees God face-to-face. The human experience of God is inevitably partial. God is revealed to us only incompletely—and as that which eludes definition.

Without such safeguards, mixing biblical literalism with the spiritual teaching the God is personally present to us yields an explosively dangerous mixture. Early in the twentieth century, the Christian "Fundamentalist" movement, with its active hostility both to scholarship and to cultural criticism, invited a genuinely dangerous projection of "divine authority" onto its own hostile ethnocentricity and its own unconsciously mechanistic theology of Jesus' rescuing us from an angry, vindictive God. But such misrepresentations of Christian spirituality do not discredit the real thing, just as creationist museums do not discredit evolutionary biology.

As anthropologist T. H. Luhrman has documented both in the *New York Times* and in her book *When God Talks Back* (2012), there are corners of Christian tradition today that completely disregard thousands of years of theological safeguards against the temptation to project unconscious content onto God. For some people, she insists, these charismatic evangelical congregations have provided joy and hope amidst life's difficulties. She insists that the congregations she studied do make an honest effort to guard against psychopathology.

Nonetheless, the deeper, more ancient traditions of Christian spirituality would caution that their way of teaching about the "personal presence" of God is an invitation to disaster. Some people might find joy and hope. But others will be both psychologically and spiritually damaged when God fails to cure cancer or provide a job or whatever specific outcome has been prayed for at such length and with such trusting fervor.

A friend told me in despair that her brother died in outrage and grief that the God whom he trusted was refusing to cure his cancer. His children would be left fatherless, his wife alone and in difficult financial circumstances. His dying was bad enough. His sense of betrayal made it all the more difficult for everyone—including him. He had no doubt whatsoever that God could have restored him to perfect health at any moment. Some preacher somewhere, I thought, should have been sued for malpractice.

Luhrman also explains that charismatic-evangelical theology can lead to the taking of public political positions without regard for ordinary standards of logic and evidence. They think that God himself has told them: no mere human critique of their positions makes any difference at all. Here too, the dangers are obvious.

The belief that God is "personally present" is a symbolic claim, not an invitation to turn the elusive sacred "presence" into either a political lobbyist or a BFF. No incredulous agnostic, snorting in contempt of the practices Luhrman recounts, could be matched in outrage by classic Christian spiritual sources. Spiritual traditions don't last for thousands of years by peddling dangerous nonsense— even if it provides, transiently, some comfort to some few.

And so I want next to examine one key portion of the biblical evidence for the claim that all statements about God are necessarily symbolic statements. Let the record show that the claim "all statements about God are symbolic statements" is *a biblical claim*. It's not my claim, it's not recent, it's not remotely postmodern.[1] It's as biblical a claim as any claim out there anywhere. In this key passage, God is defined as beyond definition. God is known only as

---

1. On the concept of symbolism in the ancient world, see Struck, *Birth of the Symbol* and my discussion of how the ancient world interpreted texts in *Confronting Religious Absolutism,* chapter 7.

the Unknowable. On that point Jews and Christians have agreed for thousands of years.

This key passage is a snippet of dialogue early in Moses's long argument with the burning bush (Exodus, chapters three and four). In this key bit of dialogue, Moses asks two pointed and somewhat sarcastic questions. The bush offers two equally swift comebacks. Its answers define both the nature of God and the character of God's personal relationship with Moses, with the Israelites, and with all who claim spiritual descent from them. It is *the* classic text for the crucial, ancient claim that, despite the vivid experience of God's personal presence, *we have no direct knowledge of God and we must never speak as if we do.*

A thousand years after Moses, in 270 BCE, this little exchange was translated from the original Hebrew into Greek. In 400 CE, the Greek was translated into Latin. Beginning with John Wycliffe in the 1300s, and then Myles Coverdale and William Tyndale in the 1500s, and then definitively in 1608, the Bible was translated into English. With each translation, the poetic elegance of the original Hebrew was more deeply obscured. God was redefined philosophically as an essentially Platonic philosophical proposition (I'll get back to that translation history later on). In what follows here I will dispute the usual English translation because I disagree with that Platonized definition of God as a philosophical proposition.

As I will explain shortly, I object to the usual translation of what the bush said because I think it destroys the narrative structure of the scene. Be aware, please, that I am making a major claim here. I'm disputing how a key line has been translated for more than two thousand years and by every major English translation for the last four hundred years. And—full disclosure—I am not a biblical scholar. Nor am I a credentialed academic theologian.

I am a literary critic. *As a literary critic* I have every right to analyze the literary structure of a dramatic scene. Be persuaded or not, then, on literary grounds or for literary reasons. Christian humanism from the 1300s onward asserted the legitimacy of my distinctively literary and cultural-history approach to Christian tradition. This approach reveals aspects of texts that other approaches do not reveal. Literary criticism as a discipline is perfectly comfortable with the fact that the original text is always "more" than what any particular reading of the text reveals. And yet, by talking intelligently about *our own experiences of the text* we help one another to have to have a richer, fuller *experience of the text.* That's all. That's the goal. The goal is not to substitute explications for the original text. (Neither will film criticism ever substitute for films themselves, nor music criticism for concerts.) As I see it, much of the problem with Christianity today is its tendency to substitute theology for immediate experience, whether that's the human experience of spiritual realities or the experience of reading our brilliant heritage of poetry and storytelling.

And so, consider yourself forewarned. For better for worse, I am not a "church" authority of any variety whatsoever.

Heeding the Poets of God

Here's what's at stake in how this scene is translated. Historically speaking, translating the elusive inner experience of the presence of God into God the Proposition is what earlier I called "theological literalism." It's an error parallel to the error of biblical literalism. As biblical literalism creates massive but unnecessary conflict with contemporary sciences (biology, geology, astrophysics, etc.) so also theological literalism creates massive and equally unnecessary conflicts with contemporary humanities (philosophy, cultural history, language and literature studies, and so forth).

Theological literalism generates the controlling God of a controlling orthodoxy. It creates both God the Superhero and God the Engineer Almighty. These characters are not viable. They are not viable conceptually. They are not viable morally. Above all, they are not viable spiritually. Disputing the standard translation will, in effect, undercut the theological absolutism of those who speak for God in a brash and inappropriately confident manner, as if they have been chosen as press secretary for an Almighty who remains hidden away in some divine Oval Office, speaking to no one else at all.

But refuting God the Proposition is only part of what's at stake. I'm much more interested in another aspect of the issue at hand: the status of the arts and the role of the moral imagination. What's really at stake here is reclaiming the Bible as a masterpiece of the moral imagination.

Here's my key claim: if anything anyone can ever say about God is necessarily and inescapably metaphoric, then the best theologians will be drawn from the tribe of poets. I mean "poets" in the root sense of the Greek word *poietes*, which means "maker." The "poet" in this classically comprehensive use of the word means "the artist" broadly defined.

The tribe of *poietes* includes storytellers, songwriters, and filmmakers. It includes both musicians and composers. It includes anyone working in a visual media: painters, sculptors, weavers, needleworkers, metalworkers, potters, photographers, videographers, and so forth. The poet classically defined is the *maker* in any media, and theologically speaking it is in our creativity that we most nearly resemble God. Or as Coleridge insisted centuries ago, imagination is and provides the human relationship to the Holy One.

Those rightly called *poietes* are they whose claim *this is true* is always and necessarily made in what I call "the lyric voice." Strictly speaking, the "lyric" is a poem expressing individual and often quite intensely personal experience. It is, thus, the voice arising from the liminal inward terrain wherein we find that the sacred is present to us. But not only the sacred, of course: on this inward terrain we encounter many kinds and varieties of profoundly true but utterly elusive truth. As a result, the primary speech of the lyric voice— whether it's "God-talk" or not—is always masterfully symbolic in whatever way is appropriate to the media at hand. *This*—whatever this is, in the chosen media—*this* is like unto *that*, which is barely accessible to us in the far liminal reaches of consciousness, at the border between body and mind. Symbolism provides our only access to our own most crucial insights into the human condition.

Those who have the talent and the self-discipline necessary to develop a clear lyric voice thereby also have the technical skill to say *this is true* and to convince us of that truth—but without that arrogant corollary *agree or be damned.* (When art gets arrogant like that, it has ceased to be art. It has become propaganda.) The great artwork evokes and elicits the production of other art, just as the great scientific experiment is one which elicits a torrent of subsequent fruitful research. The imagination is always fructifying in that way. Creativity sets loose creativity. It does not silence it.

And the Bible is, *par excellence*, the literary masterpiece of the moral imagination in the Jewish and subsequent Christian traditions. Many people have always said that Western literary and arts traditions are incomprehensible unless one has a basic understanding of the Bible. That's true. But by equal measure it demonstrates that the Bible is more than a source of something like clip art for illustrating propositional claims drawn from creeds, doctrines, dogmas, committee reports, and position papers.

"Proof-texting," it's called: quoting a sentence here and a sentence there from texts written by different people decades to centuries distant from one another, and then weaving these snippets into a single new fabric without any regard for what the sentences said in their own textual, historical, and cultural contexts. Proof-texting a one-volume literary anthology would be like taking one sentence from Shakespeare, two from Hemingway, a line and a half from Chaucer, a phrase from Allen Ginsberg, a long incantatory sentence from Walt Whitman, and a subordinate clause from Henry James. If you want to assemble a thematic discussion of some issue on such a basis, you are certainly free to do so. But you cannot then claim any authority *beyond your own* for what you have concocted.

The danger here is that some people do claim absolute authority, *divine* authority in fact, for whatever they have cut and pasted together. For an example of what it takes to restore these snippets to their original contexts, take a look at my analysis of the famous biblical lines condemning gay relationships (*Confronting Religious Denial of Gay Marriage,* chapter 6). Or my discussion of Jesus's teachings about nonviolence in *The Confrontational Wit of Jesus,* chapter 8. And professional biblical scholarship goes into far more detail—and far more highly technical detail—than I do.

Nonetheless, a simple literary close reading is both fun and fascinating. And so, heads up, ladies and gentlemen: we heading off into more of it. The next chapter will be a long one by my usual standards, but by the usual measure of average reading speeds, it will ask only eight to thirteen minutes of your time. Even if it takes half an hour because you keep slowing down to think and to evaluate critically, I think that's not too much to ask: tradition regards these lines as the Bible's single most important statement about the character and identity of God.

And let me tell you, Moses's back talk to this strange little bush is a *great* story. Did it happen as an historical event? Frankly, my dear, I don't give a damn. It is true in the fully lyrical sense. It is true as visionary poetry is true.

And that's the most enduring truth we have. It outlasts empires.

8

Moses Debates with a Burning Bush

In the original Hebrew, the text I want to examine from the book of Exodus defines or portrays God *not* as a fixed proposition (the uncaused cause or the ground of being) but rather as an essentially dynamic and forward-looking presence. He promises to accompany the Israelites into an open-ended future as they seek a quality of human society that does not yet exist anywhere. The quality of community at stake is a necessary foundation for Jesus' later and quite original claim that God is nonviolent despite an immense heritage of scriptural texts depicting God as in fact savagely violent at times.

Here's the immediate backstory to the scene in question. The Israelites are the descendants of Abraham's grandson Jacob, who was renamed Israel, a name which means both "he struggles with God" and "may God prevail." Jacob has a dozen sons, each of whom is patriarch of one of the twelve tribes of Israel. At one point, these men and their families migrated to Egypt to escape drought in their homeland. Now, generations later, their descendants have been enslaved by the Egyptians.

Moses is an Israelite. But he was secretly adopted as an infant by an Egyptian princess, daughter of the Pharaoh, and raised as her son. She knows from the outset that he is an Israelite, but does Moses himself? That's not clear: the text can be read either way. (And baby boys were not yet circumcised among the Jews: that came later.) This uncertainty about what Moses knows about himself is part of the dramatic tension shaping the snippet of dialogue I want to examine.

As an adult, Moses kills an Egyptian slave driver whom he sees abusing Israelite slaves. Pharaoh learns of this and seeks to kill him. Moses flees to Midian, marries a Midianite woman, and settles down to tending her father's flocks. The Midianites, we are told, see him as an Egyptian.

One day he spots a bush that burns brightly but is not consumed by the fire. He comes closer to take a look. A voice from within the bush tells him to take off his shoes because he is standing on holy ground. Moses does so. Then the voice from within the bush identifies itself as the God of his ancestors. It says it has heard the cries of the enslaved Israelites. It tells Moses to return to Egypt to lead the Israelites to freedom in a land this voice promises to give them.

That's the moment at which I want to pick up the dialogue between the bush and Moses: Exodus, chapter 3, verses 11–15. This passage both reflects and defines a belief that God is a personal presence in our lives—but it defines that presence in remarkably subtle ways.

I will be using the New Revised Standard Version (NRSV) translation, but I've made two big changes. First, I have re-formatted the dialogue to match how contemporary novels format dialogue. That makes it easier to see the swift back and forth here, whose implicit tensions I want to unpack for your consideration.

Second, I have consistently translated the verb *ehyeh* as "I will be." The NRSV translation follows scholarly practice generally: in the lines where God gives his name, the literal Hebrew *I will be* is ordinarily translated as *I am*. (The NRSV does provide the literal translation in a footnote.) Translating *ehyeh* as "I am" at this point is a theologically laden choice of remarkable cultural complexity.

I acknowledge the great and venerable authority of the thinking that went into this choice. Nonetheless, I think that it obscures a centrally important literary pattern in the passage, a literary pattern that also has theological significance. (I'll get back to translation history in the next chapter.)

Translations follow a second convention which I will also follow—but more consistently. In key line giving God's name, the verb *ehyeh* is translated into English set in all caps and in a smaller font, LIKE THIS. I will do so as well—but for every instance of the word *ehyeh*. This all-caps smaller-font tradition is also used for the Hebrew word *yhwh*, which is another of God's proper names. (The name is *yhwh* not *Yhwh* because Hebrew does not capitalize anything.) Jewish tradition forbade speaking aloud this sacred name, which is translated into English as Yahweh or (in the 1608 King James translation, Jehovah). Many translations, in deference to Jewish practice, substitute THE LORD, which is what a pious Jew would say when reading the text aloud. "Lord," by itself, was a term of polite address to an adult male, like "sir" or "mister." *The* lord, however, referred to the king. Where the Hebrew text says *yhwh*, I will follow the NRSV usage and say THE LORD. All of this matters because *yhwh* and *ehyeh* are both forms of the same verb stem, *hwh*.

I'll get back to *hwh* later. First let's do an initial read-through of this snippet of dialogue. As you read, keep an eye open for the multiple references to travel or journey: going, sending, bringing, and so forth. Note, furthermore, that this journey is never a solitary endeavor. It is to be a going *with*, sending *to*, bringing *with*, and so forth. Above all, watch for repetitions of that key phrase, "I will be." Let's watch:

> But Moses said to God, "Who am I that I should go to Pharaoh, and bring the Israelites out of Egypt?"
>
> He said, "I WILL BE with you; and this shall be the sign for you that it is I who sent you: when you have brought the people out of Egypt, you shall worship God on this mountain."
>
> But Moses said to God, "If I come to the Israelites and say to them, 'The God of your ancestors has sent me

to you,' and they ask me, 'What is his name?' what shall
I say to them?'

God said to Moses, "I WILL BE WHO I WILL BE."

He said further, "Thus you shall say to the Israelites,
'I WILL BE' has sent me to you."

God also said to Moses, "Thus you shall say to the
Israelites, 'THE LORD, the God of your ancestors, the God
of Abraham, the God of Isaac, and the God of Jacob, has
sent me to you'":

This is my name for ever,
and this my title for all generations." (Exod 3:11–15,
NRSV)

Let's go back over this dialogue statement by statement, unpacking the narrative tensions, the imagery, and the relevant cultural
context.

First, then, when the bush tells Moses to rescue the Israelites,
notice that Moses does not react deferentially. He does not bow and
obey instantly. He has a question.

"Who am I," he asks, "that I should that I should go to Pharaoh, and bring the sons of Israel out of Egypt?"

"I will be with you," the bush replies. That is the plainest possible translation of the Hebrew: *ehyeh* [I will be] *immak* [with you].
I've checked twenty-one different translations: that's what all of
them say.

Let's stop here for a moment. What does the bush mean by
that reply?

What Does the Bush Mean?

There are two different ways to think about what the bush means
when it says, "I will be with you." We have to keep both interpretations in mind *simultaneously* if we are to understand the drama of
this scene, just as we have to remember that Moses may or may
not have known prior to this moment that he is himself Israelite.
Maybe the bush is saying, in effect, "It doesn't matter who you
are, you schlemiel; I'm with you and that's all that counts." That

possibility underscores God's power and God's determination to free the Israelites.

If that's the case here—if Moses is an insignificant instrument of the will of God Almighty—then the speed and daring of his first comeback seem all the more bold: here's an ordinary Joe giving some lip to the Almighty. He doesn't just cringe and set out immediately to do what God commands. He says, in effect, *why are you asking me?* In Homer or in Ovid, none of the gods get this kind of back talk from humans. That says something remarkable about Moses. It also says something remarkable about the voice from the bush: why is Moses not burned to a crisp in an instant for challenging the divine command? Here is a divinity who genuinely engages with humanity.

❧

There is another possible reading of what the bush says at this point, a second possibility boiling out from within the dramatic tensions I have just described. Maybe God is saying, "I'll tell you who you are, you skeptic: you are someone to whom I am always present."

This second possibility also ties back neatly to what the bush said at first: I am the god of your ancestors. As the descendent of Abraham, Isaac, and Jacob, Moses inherits their clan god, now present to him in the burning bush.

But keep in mind, of course, that Moses does not know the book of Genesis (he hasn't written it yet). And so from Moses's perspective, the voice within the burning bush is merely claiming to be the guardian spirit of Abraham's descendants. Or maybe that's what it is *pretending* to be. Deceptive spirits were an ordinary part of the ancient world. These malevolent characters were the spiritual equivalent of phishing emails saying that you have won the lottery in Liberia and all we need to send the money is a little information. They were a commonplace security risk.

Who knows who this bush is? Moses doesn't. And maybe he is smart enough to recognize that fact.

If we are to enter fully into the drama of this scene, we need to remember that Moses has no idea what he is dealing with here. *We do.* We have already seen the prequel to this scene, so to speak. And its sequel, for that matter. Moses has not. He is wisely suspicious and intelligently cautious. And possibly a bit lippy besides.

◆

Moses's next comeback is even more dramatically unexpected: once again he reacts with an edgy question rather than murmuring some deferential assent. He asks, "If I come to the Israelites and say to them, 'The god of your ancestors has sent me to you,' and they ask me, 'What is his name?' what shall I say to them?" (And note, here, that Moses says "your ancestors" rather than "our ancestors.")

Presumably the Israelites know the name of their own clan god. What's going on here? Once again there are two very obvious choices. *If we assume that Moses does not know he is Israelite himself,* then perhaps he simply does not know the name of the Israelite god. Perhaps he is simply asking information. Possibly he is preparing for the Israelites to check his authenticity by asking for the name.

That interpretive possibility makes excellent logical sense, but it does not make dramatic sense: literary dialogue is never used for trivial questions of fact. And as a literary tradition, Hebrew narrative is very centrally dependent upon dialogue. They don't waste a word of dialogue. Never. Not a word of it. So if Moses looks as if he is asking a mundane question of fact, then in dramatic terms the question is a setup. Surely you have seen characters in movies ask innocent-sounding questions that are in fact a ploy. That's going on here too. The question is a ploy *and furthermore we are supposed to recognize that it's a ploy.*

What's really going on here? Plenty. First: remember how old this story is. Scholars locate it roughly on the cusp between the late Bronze Age and the very early Iron Age—1250 BCE or so. At that point, culturally speaking, names had power. To know the true name of a person, or a place, or a thing was to lay claim to it in some regard or perhaps even to assert control over it. At the very least, knowing a name provided powerful insight into the identity of the thing named. We see that belief echoed in Scripture every time the narrator stops to explain the relevance of a name.

A bit of this ancient tradition remains visible even in English, in surnames like Taylor, Carpenter, Baker, or Hunter. Hunters and carpenters, for instance, are apt to be very different people from tailors and bakers. Or in more potent ways yet, consider the familiar albeit controversial tradition whereby a woman newly married surrenders her father's surname and takes the surname of her husband. Or how much energy expectant parents spend trying to select names for their child. Or this: marketing companies spend royal fortunes trying to find the best name for a product they are trying to market, lest they repeat the Chevrolet mistake of trying to market in Latin American a vehicle called the "Nova." (*Nova* translates into Spanish as "it doesn't go.") In short, names *still* matter, even today. And how we feel about names does not hold a candle to the power ascribed to names in Iron Age. Names had inherent meaning.

Back to Moses, then. Is Moses being wily here in asking the bush for its name? Is he trying to get a handle on the fire? He certainly is. In fact, his ancestor Jacob tries the same trick in Genesis, chapter 32. Jacob doesn't get away with it, and neither will Moses—well, not exactly. But we need to recognize the ploy if we are to appreciate the narrative tension engendered by the question. The bush will in the end give Moses its name—in fact, three versions of its name—but while giving over the divine name it nonetheless eludes control. It lays claim to a dramatic indeterminacy. You have to recognize Moses's ploy *as a ploy* in order to appreciate the witty indeterminacy of the bush's answer. Moses does not get a handle on the fire.

And neither do we, although for thousands of years translators have tried to.

Moses's Implicit Skepticism

Furthermore, Moses is not simply being wily in asking for a name. I think there is also an undercurrent of sarcasm. We need to hear that too, or we will fail to appreciate why the bush responds both thunderously *and* in the very specific way that it does.

The implicit content of Moses's question might be paraphrased something like this: "oh, so you are the god of the Israelites—the god who failed to keep them out of this slavery mess, eh? Who *are* you, anyhow?"

After all, the major item in the job description of a god was protecting his people. At this point, the god of Abraham, Isaac, and Jacob has failed to meet that standard. Now he is claiming to have the power to liberate them? Indirectly, through Moses, rather than in person? Gods usually do their own work. If this bush wants the Israelites freed, why doesn't he deal in person with Pharaoh and with Pharaoh's gods? And where has he *been* all this time? We have to see the improbability of what the bush is saying if we are to un-pack and appreciate the narrative tension of this scene. (And we might note, in that regard, Jesus' later appearance as yet another improbable human figure through whom God becomes dramati-cally present. The Gospel of Matthew establishes a wide array of Moses–Jesus parallels.)

Moses's acute skepticism is perfectly reasonable. He is, re-member, a refugee from an enslaved people subjected to a geno-cidal ploy by their owners. He is out here "beyond the wilderness," we are told, tending another man's flocks. By the usual standards for adult males, he is something of a failure: he is subordinate to his wife's father, not head of his own household. He is also a des-perately isolated figure. There was real poignancy buried within his first question, "Who am I?" He is not exactly Jewish, not exactly Egyptian, not exactly Midianite. He has already taken an immense spiritual journey, from his birth among the Israelites, to the Pha-raoh's palace, to the construction sites where slaves are abused, to life on the lam as a criminal, to the Midianites, and now, finally, out here "beyond the wilderness." He is beyond the beyond, out here alone with animals, almost as if he has become something less than fully human himself. A Cain figure, perhaps, banished for murder? The poignancy of his personal situation adds dramatic tension to his two sharply parallel questions: "who am I?" and "who are *you*?"

Stop for a moment here and imagine that you are directing an actor playing the part of Moses. What tone of voice would you want? What physical demeanor? Remember that Moses killed a man: he's a physical guy. Later he will have a whole catalogue of rea-sons why he's the wrong man for the job. Is that pushback insecurity and depression? Shrewd judgment? Raw courage even in the face of a god? We need to fill in some blanks here, and above all we have to be conscious of and accountable for how we do so. Obviously one can't imagine Moses fully on the basis of this small exchange, not given the length of the entire Moses saga. But we have to at least ask those questions before we can begin to answer them—because answer them we must, sooner or later, in a full "reading" of the Moses saga. More to the point, perhaps, we all have implicit or unconscious assumptions about Moses's demeanor even here, at the outset. It's worth pausing to make yours conscious. Please take a moment to do so.

The bush has three replies in rapid succession. And if I were the director here, I'd call in the special effects folks to make the bush flare up in a tower of flame at this point. That would be a nice foreshadowing of the pillar of fire that leads the escaping Israelites through the wilderness at night (Exod 13:29). But it's equally appropriate to the forcefulness of how the bush answers: it identifies itself to Moses with three different names.

The bush's three versions of God's names constitutes one of the most hyper-explicated and contentiously translated little passages in all of Scripture. If literary critics had some equivalent of removing their shoes, that's what I should do before continuing.

The Bush Replies: The Three Names of God

Although this passage is prose, it has a visibly poetic structure. The triplet of names reflects the usual form of poetry in Hebrew.[1] That is, Hebrew poetry is written in couplets or triplets in which each subsequent line in some way mirrors the first line. But the apparent "repetition" or mirroring among lines is never *exactly* repetition: each time around, there is a slight change of meaning.

The change might be delicate and witty. It might be sharp and bitter. It might be subtle and heartbreaking. It might escalate disappointment into despair, or move despair to hope. It might trace subsequent moments in a dramatic action, or play logical options

---

1. On the forms of poetry in Hebrew, see Alter, *The Art of Biblical Poetry*, and Kugel, *The Great Poems of the Bible*.

off one another. It might confirm conventional wisdom or defy it boldly. The wordplay is commonly both poetically brilliant and theologically loaded. So when the bush offers in rapid succession three different formulations of God's name, we need to be very alert. Subsequent tradition certainly has been alert: that's why there is so much at stake in how these three verses are translated.

If you will, please imagine that these three repetitions of God's name are like pop-up windows that open in response to Moses's question. All three must remain open simultaneously. Furthermore: within each window there will be an allusion to something else, an allusion that functions more or less as a hotlink functions. We will be opening those hotlinks too, just briefly, just long enough to get the relevant allusions clear in our minds.

Here are the three major pop-up windows.

(1) "God said to Moses, I WILL BE WHO I WILL BE. [*ehyeh aser ehyeh*]."

(2) He said further, "Thus you shall say to the Israelites, 'I WILL BE [*ehyeh*] has sent me to you.'"

(3) God also said to Moses, "Thus you shall say to the Israelites, 'THE LORD God [*yhwh elohim*] of your ancestors has sent me to you.'"

Let's look at each of these names in turn.

The First Name: I will be who I will be.

The first name of God, literally translated as *I will be who I will be*, resonates powerfully back to the creation scene in Genesis. The deity who created the cosmos by saying "let there *be*" has no single essence or determinative identity. Its potent creativity applies exponentially to its own identity: in the future it will be whatever it blessed well chooses to be. (Or, if you prefer, it will come in time to reveal whatever further dimensions of its identity it wants to reveal.)

The usual presumption, as I said before, is that we are discovering something new about God, not that God is actually changing. But from the human side, the two logical possibilities implicit in

"I will be who I will be" are functionally equivalent: we can't tell whether God is *changing* or whether God is *revealing* something new that has been there all along, either invisible or unnoticed. As a result, whatever we know is simply whatever we know *at the moment*. Our knowledge of God is never complete nor final nor absolute, because we have no way to know what God in God's creative fecundity will either come to *be* or come to *reveal* to us.

Can God Change?

There's a very nifty text classically cited as an example of either "God changing his mind" or the community changing its perception of God and thus, because the experience of God is personified in a literary way, the narrative character named *God* "changes his mind."[2] It's a tale in the book of Numbers from the exodus journey from Egypt to the promised land. God decrees a census of male Israelites over the age of twenty who would be suitable as warriors (Num 26:2). Acreage in the promised land is to be distributed equally on the basis of this head count (Num 26:52–56).

But there's a problem. There are five unmarried sisters whose father has died (Num 27:1–11). They step up to dispute the patrilineal distribution of land because it will leave them landless. And God says, "The daughters of Zelophehad are right: you shall give them possession of an inheritance among their father's brethren and cause the inheritance of their father to pass to them" (Num 27:7). And so it is done. God also adapts his previous decree about land distribution to allow for similar situations in the future.

But there's still a problem. If one of these sisters were to marry a man from another tribe, their inheritance through their father would eventually pass to that tribe. The male cousins of these five

2. I am delighted here to acknowledge Congregation Beit Simchat Torah and the following lay sermon by their member Roberta Kaplan, JD, who represented Eddie Windsor in the Supreme Court case in which the Defense of Marriage Act was held unconstitutional: http://www.youtube.com/watch?v=_5nNJK3B56Y This link was sent to me at an exquisitely perfect moment by my friend Richard Batdorf, JD. Thanks to him too. I have a special guardian angel assigned to lofting unexpected resources onto my desk, so help me I do. Thanks to her as well.

sisters object because they do not want their tribal-heritage land accruing to a different tribe.

And so God changes God's original decree a second time (Num 36:1–10). The *principle* of social justice and economic equality holds, just as the principle of marital fidelity holds in gay marriage. But the decrees of THE LORD can and do adapt in response to unintended consequences and unforeseen circumstances—which is to say, the law of a just God will judiciously adapt to exigencies that develop over time *and in response to human arguments about injustice.* (Furthermore, the theological "content" of the episode does not depend upon its historicity one way or another. The episode can be *narrative theology*—doing theology by telling a story—rather than historical chronicle.)

In short, the idea that *what God has decreed* can never be changed is predicated upon a God who never changes. That's the God of Plato, not the God of Abraham, Isaac, and Jacob. (In the next chapter I will have more to say about Platonic influence on biblical translations.)

The Second Name of God: "I will be has sent me"

Now let's turn to the second name. It goes like this: "Thus you shall say to the Israelites, 'I WILL BE has sent me to you.'" What's *that* getting at?

I see that name as an allusion back to what the bush said in the immediately prior exchange. When Moses asked, "Who am I that I should go to Pharaoh?," God replied, "I WILL BE with you." Now Moses is told to tell the people that I WILL BE has sent him.

That is—as I see it—Moses is to tell the people that the God who is with *him* will be with *them* as well. And the proof that God *is* with them is that God has sent *Moses* to be with them and to lead them out of slavery—out here "beyond the wilderness" to this same mountain, where they will worship God.

At that point, of course, they will receive from God a body of law defining a human community in which the bounty of the earth is shared appropriately, immigrants and outsiders are never exploited as the Israelite have been exploited, and the needs of the poor are never forgotten. As we saw a minute ago, the promised land is also to be divided into equal plots of land. In an agrarian society—this is an Iron Age story, remember—that's a radically egalitarian division of wealth. And according to the sacred law given to Moses, this distribution of wealth is to be regularly restored if it becomes distorted over time.

In the twenty-first century as in the Iron Age, that was a radical socioeconomic vision. Scholars debate whether or to what extent the Israelite community practiced this mandated redistributions of wealth, forgiveness of debt, and so forth. How much was visionary poetry and how much was concrete property rights? I'm not equipped even to guess.

But I can say this: the visionary poetry of a community—its sacred Scriptures—certainly do matter. Our moral ideals matter even when we fail to embody them perfectly or consistently. It matters for American culture, for instance, that our founding documents declare all of us equal and endowed with rights that no one can ever abridge. It's crucial to realize, then, that the promised land is not simply real estate and economic regulations of real estate. It is also a powerful moral vision of how human society ought to be organized: no one should ever go hungry. Nobody gets to profit by poisoning someone else's water. *As a moral vision,* these beliefs have had concrete historical consequences.

As I read this snippet, the Israelites are being "sent" out of slavery and "sent" on their way into this moral-imaginative vision of human community just as (and because) Moses is being "sent" to them in an equally improbable undertaking. I think that if we fail to recognize the improbability of both endeavors, then we fail to see what this passage is trying to say about the character of this equally improbable God. The gods of surrounding nations do not care about landless daughters, abused slaves, socioeconomic exploitation, or agricultural practices to protect the soil. But THE LORD God does. As I explain in more detail in *Confronting Religious Violence,* chapter 3, the gods of the ancient world overwhelmingly sacralized the power of the reigning elite. They did not side with the downtrodden. As gods go, THE LORD God is one very quirky character.

God is, in effect, choosing to exercise his self-defining free-dom to *become* the God who will be present to the Israelites, lead-ing/sending them out of slavery and accompanying them into an equally open, equally dramatic journey toward a quality of human community that no one anywhere has fully realized. On that jour-ney—on that "journey"—God establishes a national covenant with the people. Because they were rescued from slavery, they are to create a society shaped by its commitment to distributive socioeco-nomic justice, which is to say a deep concern for those who have least.

Will they consistently succeed? Obviously not. But remaining faithful to the ideal matters, just as it matters to remain faithful to a divinity who is only imperfectly known.

The Third Name of God: Yahweh God

Now let's look at the bush's third formulation of God's name. It is thunderously traditional: for us, the hotlink here opens a window to the entire biblical history of THE LORD God. But as I said before: Moses doesn't know any of that history yet. What *we* know about THE LORD God is not, at this point, what Moses knows about his bush. In fact, later God tells Moses that even Abraham, Isaac, and Jacob never knew that God's proper name is "Yahweh" (Exod 6:3). ("God," of course, is a generic noun, like "dog" or "cat." Then and now, there are thousands of particular gods. Each has a proper name—Zeus, Shiva, Ganesha, Gaia, or, for the Jews and later Chris-tians, Yahweh.) Moses is told to reveal to the Israelites the proper name of God—the deep identity of God—when he tells them "THE LORD God of your ancestors, the God of Abraham, the God of Isaac, and the God of Jacob, has sent me to you" (Exod 3:15a).

And then the bush adds something, a comment directed sim-ply at Moses: "this is my name for ever, and this is my title for all generations." *What*, exactly, is God's title for all generations? Merely THE LORD God? I think not. I think that the literary force of cou-plets and triplets in Hebrew tradition demands either rough equiv-alence among the God's three answers or, commonly, an escalation among roughly equivalent terms. And so, I'd argue, "God's name" poetically speaking is all three names: I WILL BE WHO I WILL BE, plus I WILL BE with you and sending you and leading you, plus THE LORD God. The proper name "THE LORD God" is to operate as a summary of all three names—and furthermore as a permanent allusion to this particular scene and to the complex plan God has in mind. The intensely creative God of Genesis is at it again here, creating something new within his existing creation.

And now consider this: both the proper name *yhwh* (or Yahweh) and the verb *ehyeh* ("I will be") derive from the same verb stem, *hwh*. The Hebrew verb *hwh* is translated into English as "to be, to become, and to come to pass," which is why translators are not making some kind of obvious mistake, later, when they translate "I will be" as "I am." Here's the issue: strictly speaking, Hebrew has no verb equivalent to our verb "to be." (Many languages don't, in fact. Russian, for instance.) The Hebrew verb stem *hwh* always has the strong forward-looking slant of *to become* or *to come to pass*. And so, I'd argue, the poetic logic of deriving the names of God from the stem *hwh* strongly suggests that this is not a God willing to be frozen in the past. He is not some Iron Age artifact who belongs in a plexiglass case in some museum. That is not what he tells Moses about who he is. As the story unfolds, we realize even more dramatically that THE LORD God is doing something quite unprecedented vis-à-vis the ordinary behavior of gods in the ancient world.

And so, THE LORD God, fiery and self-defined as beyond all definition, is portrayed in this key text as both intensely forward-looking and intensely dynamic as he sends the Israelites off into an entirely new future. We are never to think we have a handle on this fire. It cannot be grasped. It will be whatever it will be, endlessly and evermore both beyond us and out in front of us, that pillar of fire calling us forward—a sacred reality before which we should remove our shoes. To revert to an astute coinage of William Tyndale, a vitally important sixteenth-century translator, the name of God in English is not the static Platonic I AM but the utterly dynamic I WILBE, a spelling displaced just enough from the familiar to remind us that this God eludes our efforts at definition.

In the long conversation between Moses and his burning bush, encompassing all the rest of chapter three and all of chapter four besides, the word "will" echoes and re-echoes: God says over and over again, "I will do this" and "I will do that." *I will do,* just as *I will be.* And when Moses complains that he is inarticulate, God says "I WILL BE with your mouth," a dynamic presence within him, guiding him through the difficult process of liberation.

The fire of the burning bush is also within us, as the personal presence of God is within us: the light of intellect, the perceptive warmth of compassion, the dangerous fire of creativity, an ability that humanity has used both for great evil and for great good. The God who is I WILL BE challenges us to decide in turn whom *we* will be. What choices will *we* make?

You don't have to believe in the reality of THE LORD God to feel that your choices in life have an inescapable moral significance. Regardless of religious or political allegiances, and probably as part of our hard-wired sociability, all of us both possess and seek lives of moral substance. My point here, my larger point, is that we inherit from the Jews and through the followers of Jesus a complex, fascinating tradition. It has struggled for thousands of years to grapple honestly with the question, "What will *I* be?" As Moses asked, *who am I that you should send me?* Where are we going in our lives?

That question haunts all of us. Who am I? Why? Where am I going? Why? At the center of those incessant questions there is God, an elusive unpredictable God, the energy behind those questions.

The Copernican turn of Christian humanism claims that all of Christian tradition, every last ounce of it, is an effort to articulate and to explore the human moral experience of grappling with this consummately disconcerting God. And within this Copernican turn there is a further turn, a quantum turn, an inescapable, minimally understood paradox: the sacred, however you wish to define it, is a vivid, personally present reality within our deepest experience, but it is a reality about which we can speak only indirectly and only symbolically. A God who can be known only as I WILL BE cannot be trapped in nets of finely precise philosophical constructions by systematic theologians—although heaven knows they have tried.

We all try. I'm guilty of that too. What else have I been doing here but trying to explain to you the actual identity of THE LORD God portrayed in these gloriously complex old stories? What is a thinker like me supposed to do when what is impossible and what is necessary converge? That paradox is at the very heart of my deeply paradoxical faith.

That blessed bush had a point. It won then, and it continues to win.

9

"I AM" v. "I WILL BE": Translation and the Authority of Theologians

Moses's famous argument with the burning bush was translated into Greek in 270 BCE. That translation was made because Greek had become the dominant international language and the dominant culture of the Mediterranean basin. Large Jewish communities all over the Mediterranean basin no longer spoke Hebrew. And so they translated their Scriptures.

In this translation, called the "Septuagint," the Hebrew sentence "I will be who I will be" was translated into Greek as "I am the one who is."

That translation proved hugely influential. And (sweeping generalization alert) it was the beginning of tendency to define God as a philosophical concept—as the great *Nous* or "Mind" of Platonic tradition. Over thousands of years, this merger of THE LORD God with the Platonic Nous yields the radically controlling Engineer Almighty, that old man in the sky, the God out there somewhere supposedly calling all the shots.

The God of the Philosophers

Equating THE LORD God with the Platonic Nous constituted a major shift in Jewish theological tradition. First, it's a shift toward the Platonic belief that the unchanging is both morally superior and intellectually superior to that which *does* change Here's the crucial assumption behind that belief: anything that changes must either become better or worse. If something is already perfect—as presumably God is perfect—then it cannot change. There is no room within such thinking for the belief that God might be dynamic, adaptable, flexible, passionately loving and compassionate, reciprocal, etc. and yet still somehow "count" as God.

Equating God with the Platonic Nous was a major theological shift in a second way as well. It redefined God as the concept of causality. That's a bit abstruse, so bear with me here for a minute. I need to bring the abstraction down to earth.

Let's start with an assumption that most of us might easily share: everything that exists has a reason for existing. My computer has a manufacture date. I have a birth date. I live in a neighborhood that did not exist until debris from the Great Fire of 1871 was bulldozed into shallow, swampy wetlands just north of the Chicago River, patted down, more landfill added, and then built upon. Earth existed only after a certain point in time that astrophysicists can more or less pinpoint, and they can more or less explain how planets were formed from star dust and gases and so forth. Cause behind cause behind cause behind cause, all the way back to the Big Bang. No one can explain what caused the Big Bang, and it's considered a vulgar misunderstanding of physics even to ask. But Big Bang theory had a beginning. It has only been physics orthodoxy for a few decades now. It may not continue to be orthodoxy.

In short, no matter what you want to name in the world around us today, it began to exist at some point. The reasons for its coming into existence can be specified. Or we trust that these reasons *can* be specified, even if we don't yet have that explanation nailed down.

The ancient world believed this causal series simply had to have a starting point. They thought that there was an obvious logical necessity for some first cause, for something that exists in and of itself and not because it was caused by something else. There has to be a starting point somewhere. That claim still has a certain commonsense appeal. Consciously or unconsciously, many people today would agree.

No matter how agreeable that assumption is to common sense, it's still an *assumption*. The actual existence of this starting point cannot be demonstrated philosophically or established scientifically. Comfortable common sense all by itself is not a rigorously adequate guide to what *must necessarily* exist.

But in the ancient world, let me repeat, this commonsense assumption was *not* questioned (on the whole). And so, over time, THE LORD God came to be defined philosophically as this starting point. God came to be understood as "Being" itself or as the "Ground of Being," and as the "Uncaused Cause" or the "First Cause." And—quite a bit later—as that which is greater than anything we can imagine.

And that's not all. God also came to defined as "The Good," the *summum bonum,* the greatest good or the highest good. In this capacity, God serves as the anchor or the warrant of the goodness of all particular things that we judge to be "good." As this argument goes, all human distinctions between good and evil depend philosophically upon the existence of something that is good *in and of itself,* beyond all human arguments, evidence, tastes, desires, opinions, cultural habits, and so forth. "The Good"—*The* Good—is thus something like the moral equivalent of the uncaused cause.

In the metaphysical world view of classical antiquity, the existence of "The Good" is the logically necessary presupposition behind any particular arguments about whether this or that proposed action is morally acceptable or not. *Of course* "The Good" exists, they thought. That's how we recognize that this or that behavior is "good." The existence of "The Good" was for the ancient world entirely self-evident.

[Philosophical sidebar: When the existence of "The Good" ceases to be a self-evident philosophical necessity in our culture, there arises the claim (falsely attributed to Dostoyevsky) that if God is dead—if "The Good" does not exist—then all things are permitted. Why are all things permitted? Because many people still feel that if "The Good" does not exist as a metaphysical anchor, then there is no logical basis for the human moral distinction between "good" and "evil." "Good" or "moral" mean only "I like it; I approve of it" and nothing more.]

Philosophical propositions like the uncaused cause, the ground of being, and the greatest good are not *proofs* of God, although sometimes they are talked about that way. Strictly speaking these propositional claims are *attributes* of God—attributes which presuppose the metaphysical substructures of the ancient world world view. One might say that THE LORD God of the Jews was drafted into filling these metaphysically necessary roles, or maybe that—shifting metaphors—after a major corporate merger between Jewish religion and Greek philosophy, these duties were simply added to his job description.

The new duties were not exactly a good fit with the character named "THE LORD God" who plays such a major role in all of these old stories. His passionate personality and deep commitment to widows and orphans seem a bit messy for a God defined as the Ground of Being and the Uncaused Cause. Those pure, cerebral, metaphysical functions also seem just a bit at odds with how Hebrew tradition defined God—as *chesed* or "loving-kindness" and as "righteousness," or pragmatic social justice. Worse yet, stories about God's occasionally savage violence would seem clearly to disqualify him as a manifestation of the *summum bonum*.

The complicated questions involved here kept both philosophers and theologians gainfully employed for centuries.

Who Converted Whom?

It's hard to know what to make of this development in Jewish theology. Is the dynamic Jewish God of loving-kindness and with-us Presence getting defined away, submerged in the increasingly Greek culture of the ancient world? Maybe influence runs the other way around. Maybe in that powerfully influential translation of Hebrew Scriptures into Greek, the Jews were saying to the ancient world, in effect, "you know that Uncaused Cause you say has to exist somewhere? We know what that is. It's not pure logic or pure rationality.

It's compassion. It's loving-kindness and it calls all of us to social justice. *Compassion is the creative force explaining why everything else exists in the first place."*

Such a claim is not astrophysics. It's poetry. And *as poetry,* as in fact visionary poetry about the deepest reality of human experience and human community, it's a daring claim indeed. Keep this possibility open in your mind, because poetic arguments of this kind or at this level are remarkably characteristic of the ancient world. They thought in metaphors. They understood—as we are slowly relearning—that *symbolism* is humanity's most sophisticated cognitive tool.

The Growing Greek Influence

The Septuagint translation reflects a long tradition of defining God in strict philosophical terms—in terms that over time yield the vast heritage of Christian dogmas, doctrines, catechisms, and the like.

Consider, for instance, Philo of Alexandria. If the Septuagint translation was step one toward redefining God as a philosophical concept, then Philo was step two. He was a learned and influential Jewish philosopher who was born about thirty years before Jesus. Philo's influence was probably at its peak in the same decades in which the Apostle Paul was writing his famous epistles.

Philo argued at length for parallels between Socrates and Moses. He offered a complex allegorical reading of Hebrew Scriptures, arguing that Moses was Socrates's major source. Like the translation into Greek, Philo proved hugely influential. He's influential both for what he himself argued and for what he shows us now about the cultural power of Greek thought in the ancient world. The Gospel of Luke in many ways picks up from Philo, presenting Jesus as a Jewish Socrates who, like Socrates himself, was executed by the state. As I mentioned earlier, the Gospel of Matthew portrays Jesus as a new Moses—which is to say, simultaneously, a new Socrates boldly confronting corrupt and ignorant elements in society.

Fast forward a few centuries. By the year 400 CE or so, Latin was displacing Greek as the international language of the region. A Bible written in Greek was becoming as problematic as a Bible written in Hebrew had been. And so Jerome translated the Greek Bible into Latin. He did so single-handedly, a rare feat. His translation was step three toward redefining God as a philosophical concept.

Jerome knew the original Hebrew text of Jewish Scriptures. But by Jerome's day, the Greek translation from 270 BCE had been *the* version of Hebrew Scripture—*even for Jews*—for almost 700 years. It had an unquestionable authority. (The Christian New Testament was written in Greek to begin with—although Jesus himself spoke Aramaic, and some of the Gospel authors were clearly not native speakers of Greek.)

Furthermore, by Jerome's day Christianity itself had become even more profoundly Greek in most regions of Rome's sprawling, rapidly dissolving empire. Jewish theological influence was both limited to a few regions and increasingly suspect within Christianity as a whole.[1] Except in areas of lingering Jewish ethnic influence, Christianity in Jerome's day was thoroughly dominated by Greek intellectual culture.

That Greek influence reflected the stature of Plotinus, a major philosopher from the 200s. Plotinus is regarded as the "father" of Neoplatonism. Plotinus defined the world view of his contemporaries no less powerfully than Einstein or Heisenberg shape ours. Einstein and Heisenberg influence our thinking even if we have never read them. They influence our thought even if we couldn't begin to follow their complex mathematics. Our firsthand ignorance of them does not diminish their cultural influence upon us. Neither did it matter much in the ancient world whether Jerome's readers had read the *Enneads* of Plotinus. Neoplatonism (including the variants now called Gnosticism) shaped the culture within which Jerome worked.

And so, it's no surprise that Jerome's Latin translation followed the Greek of the Septuagint. In doing so, he was trying to preserve and interpret the Bible in ways that would make sense to the critical thinkers of his own day. That was legitimate. In fact, he pushed the Greek translation even further in the direction of

---

1. Brown talks about this in *The Body and Society*. So does Jenkins in *Jesus Wars* and Ehrman in *Lost Christianities*.

Platonic philosophy: he translated the "I am the one who is" as "I am I"—*ego sum ego*. With that translation, THE LORD God of the Jews was unequivocally assimilated to the Plotinian One (or "The Good") or to the Platonic Nous. (Sweeping generalization alert: the Plotinian One and the Platonic Nous are not exactly equivalent.[2])

Unfortunately, Jerome's hugely influential translation—literally, I AM I—collapses the metaphor complex shaping the burning bush scene. It obscures the metaphoric references to "travel" or "journey"—and thus to freedom from oppression, injustice, and slavery. It collapses all that delicately poetic and narrative wordplay around going-with, being-with, sent-to, sent-from, travel-into, etc., that define THE LORD God as a dynamic personal presence. The dynamic, forward-gazing God who calls himself I WILL BE WHO I WILL BE becomes a static propositional claim: I am I, A = A, I am the Uncaused Cause, I am the still point on which the universe turns.

God the Propositional Claim

Here's the problem with the tendency to define God as a philosophical concept: from any propositional claim we can infer and deduce the truth of other propositional claims, and so forth in an ever-widening circle. The consequence of that can be the dogmatic illusion that we have captured in our nets the elusive reality at the center of human spiritual experiences. And *that*, in turn, invites trouble. It invites—or at least opens the door to—an ideological co-opting of religious tradition.

But we have not in fact captured God. No philosophical proposition captures the essence of that which dwells at the heart of those momentary encounters with something—and what was it? what is it?—that we instinctively recognize as "holy." Whatever this is (call it what you will), it is both more than and different from than any philosophical claim.

Ultimately, I think nothing more deeply offends nonbelievers than the arrogance with which fundamentalism insists, "Oh *we*

---

2. If you are inclined to investigate this further, one easily accessible starting point is the free online Stanford Encyclopedia of Philosophy.

know what this is. And it's *ours*. Ours *alone*, by the way. And here's the truth, Bud: you need to be *saved*, so come to church or go to hell. *Our* church, by the way. Only *our* church can save you from the wrath of God."

When poetry was translated into proposition, Christianity opened the door (however inadvertently) to such misunderstanding.

Sixteen hundred years after Jerome's lonely, single-handed, perhaps even heroic translation of the Bible into Latin, and partly in response to 2,000 years of propositional systematic theology and institutional dogmatism, English translations now follow Jerome: I AM WHO I AM, a theologically laden bit of tinkering with font sizes. Only William Tyndale (1494–1546) consistently translates the Hebrew verb *ehyeh* as *I will be*. As I said before, Tyndale coins the verb "wilbe" as a translation for *ehyeh*. "I wilbe what I wilbe," God says. That's very nice. That's the poetic heft of *ehyeh*.

In his own English translation from Jerome's Latin, Miles Coverdale (1488–1569), who did not read either Greek or Hebrew, follows Tyndale. The King James translators (1608) follow the fine poetic instincts of Tyndale and Coverdale many other places, but not here. They render the key phrase "I AM THAT I AM." They follow Jerome's Latin translation.

And on the whole, every subsequent major English translation by Christians has followed the King James. The phrase is almost always translated "I AM WHO I AM." (The New Jerusalem translation goes back to the Septuagint, translating the phrase—without fussing with fonts—as "I am he who is.") No one uses Tyndale's perfectly lovely "I wilbe what I wilbe." Alas.

The Name of God, Then and Now

A vast theological commentary on the nature of God orbits around the definition of God as that all-caps "I AM WHO I AM." In its origins, this theology was an intellectually, philosophically, and morally responsible effort to understand God within the cultural context of the ancient world. What worked then—what was necessary then—does not work now. It is not necessary. In fact, it has become problematic. Seeing that clearly, admitting it plainly, should be common sense. I contend that the essentially creative process that is religious faith has its own dynamic, evolving history akin to what is visible in art history, music history, literary history, and so forth.

Art today is not the art of the ancient world. They would not recognize some of our music as music *at all*. That fact discredits neither their music or ours. We can deeply revere our musical heritage and learn from it avidly without for a moment denying that we have our own songs to sing. So also with artistic efforts to share spiritual experiences. The fact of historical change discredits neither them nor us unless we are trapped within a static theological orthodoxy. And Christianity has at times been trapped within its own orthodoxy and within a static vision of who God is supposed to be. But if we trust the storyteller of Exodus—if we give the Bible a place of honor as *the* classic account of the human experience of God—then God is remarkably dynamic. If God is dynamic, then significant theological changes in our understanding of God are just about inevitable. Change is—at the very least—not ruled out of court *by definition*.

At our point in history, when our entire world view is so densely dynamic, I think it makes sense to reclaim the open-endedness of "I WILL BE WHO I WILL BE" as the identity of God. It makes sense to me to reclaim this ancient narrative-theology account of how a dynamic God, intimately present to us and with us, can send us out to liberate both ourselves and one another from whatever enslaves us. Doing so also makes sense in straight doctrinal terms: in defining God as "trinitarian" in nature, the creeds *(as currently interpreted)* define God as essentially dynamic and essentially relational. That's the dynamism captured by translating *ehyeh aser ehyeh* as "I WILL BE WHO I WILL BE."

But in saying "this makes sense to me," I am not insisting that I am objectively correct in how I read this scene and those who have translated it differently are all objectively wrong. I don't want to swap one rigid orthodoxy for another. That's pointless. That's not how the moral imagination works.

And so I insist: in their own cultural contexts, the Septuagint translators, Jerome, and the King James translators were not wrong. They were not wrong because they were trying to explain who God is within a culture for whom Platonism was massively important, such that radical unchangingness was a necessary feature of God-ness. They might well have been trying to push Platonism toward the compassionate, engaged, deeply present divinity known through the Jews.

It didn't work. In fact, in some ways maybe the effort backfired. But not entirely, not by a long shot. But it backfired sufficiently that we still have strands within Christianity insisting upon God's radical, timeless, unchanging character and using that theological position to underwrite both a reactionary politics and a politically dangerous religious absolutism.

Jerome set an example we need to follow. He was willing to reinterpret a heritage of ancient wisdom in the light of his own contemporary world view. Both he and the anonymous Septuagint translators set an example that I have followed here to the best of my abilities and training.

And what holds me and them and you and everyone else together in this complex, centuries-long cultural process is the incredible durability of a great story poetically told—Moses, the consummate outsider, the wanted murderer, arguing with a bush that calls him to lead a band of escaped slaves out of a genocidal enslavement and into an incredible journey toward a social vision of the just, equitable, morally sensitive human community.

That's a story that any good storyteller can retell even to an audience whose world view is shaped by quantum physics not the philosophy of Plato.

In their various ways, the sciences describe the entire cosmos as radically dynamic, from the birth of stars to the evolution of fruit flies to the behavior of subatomic particles. The claim I am making, quite simply, is that theology can change too. Christianity itself can change. It has changed already. In describing God as the dynamic I WILL BE WHO I WILL BE, Christian humanists like me are merely reading more closely our own foundational narratives.

We are simply reclaiming an ancient vision of the divine as that which accompanies us on the long human journey toward a new and more perfectly just social order.

The holy one, whatever it is exactly, is and will be whatever we need at the moment to find the courage necessary to travel out into the wilderness that is the trackless moral predicaments of our own historical moment. None of us see a clear path forward from the problems that loom over us like Egyptian slavedrivers in days of old. But *as the story goes,* a pillar of fire, the fire of divine compassion, will lead us through the night.

10

Theological Weirdness (2): The Symbolic Claim that God Is Necessarily Impersonal

The experience of God's sustaining presence—the experience re-counted so dramatically in Moses's encounter with the bush—is not the only story within Christian spirituality about the human encounter with God. There are other experiences. I want to look at these experiences carefully too, because these other experiences in effect explain how *philosophical* definition of God fits into the larger tradition of Christian spirituality.

In short, there is a nonpersonal experience of God. These experiences are just as important as the experience of God as *personally* present to us. These experiences also caution us not to take literally our perception that God is personally present. Literal-mindedness of any variety is a setup for sliding into fundamentalism.

Here's the short list of reasons why God cannot possibly be a "person." Just for starts, every person has a body. That body has gender and a richly embodied, deeply socialized brain. Our engendered bodies, our fragile, complicated brains, and our individual social experiences are all essential to our identity. Every person also has acute psychological needs. Every person has a remarkable capacity for dark, destructive emotions like jealousy, insecurity, shame, greed, rage, lust, and so forth. Every person has a vast array of unconscious needs and drives. Above all, every person is mortal, situated in time and culture, and developmentally dynamic.

None of that is true of God. None of it. Neither does God have a belly button. It's a colossal, classic, rudimentary mistake to generalize from claims that the sacred is personally present within us to assumptions that God is characterized by some irrelevant aspects of human personhood. To make that mistake is to revert to God-as-superhero anthropomorphism, an anthropomorphism that rightly earns the scorn of nonbelievers.

And so let me say again: *a symbolic claim cannot be taken literally.* To literalize, to concretize, is to collapse symbolism into nonsense. The God in whom I believe is not a cartoon character up there in the sky, that guy who is making a list, checking it twice, and planning either to admit me to heaven or to torture me endlessly in hell. That's not what honest God-talk is talking about. What believers *are* talking about is immensely more subtle. What is meant by God is not a some version of "somebody-ness."

Trying Another Metaphor on for Size

As a thought experiment, let's play for a moment with a different metaphor for God. Just as the "person" metaphor illumines the centrally important experience of being personally loved, so also God might be compared metaphorically to gravity. The love that God offers is like gravity. Gravity is not a thing. It is not an entity. We can't paint its picture or mount a statue of it on a pedestal. It's not something you can touch.

Gravity is also a relationship—most simply described as the consequence of a relationship between two bodies having mass. When we say "God," we are also naming a relationship: the relationship between "the divine" and "the human." Any time we speak of God, after all, we are speaking only of the inevitably partial human and inward experience of God, a partial and interior experience that is to some immeasurable extent culturally constructed. That's the theological equivalent of Heisenberg's Uncertainty Principle: the observer matters. Given the limits of our perceptual apparatus, there is no getting around the observer.

Just as gravity is always there, whether we are paying attention to it or not, just as gravity is not jealous when we ignore it, so also this paradoxically "impersonal" love is present, holding our spiritual feet to the ground, so to speak, whether we notice or not. A loving-kindness that is like gravity is never jealous or judgmental. It is never self-seeking nor controlling. It is not envious or irritable. It is never violent nor vindictive. It is patient; it is kind. It will never abandon us. Impersonal cosmic compassion is always there, whether or not we notice, whether or not we cultivate our ability to notice, whether or not we react.

Alternative metaphors like "gravity" offer a breath of fresh air when I start suffocating underneath the excessively literal anthropomorphism of conventional God-talk. It's also an excellent antidote to the excessive masculinity of "Heavenly Father" and "Father Almighty."

But that's not the only advantage of gravity metaphors. Gravity is a terrific image for a compassion that never descends into manipulative coercion, whining, smothering, resentment, and so forth. Any real person who loved me as unrelentingly as God does would get on my nerves in no time flat. Why? Because among human being such unrelentingness would become controlling and indeed pathological. But God is not controlling. God does not have a human ego with all that entails: God is *not* a person. As a result, the cool impersonality of the gravity metaphor is spiritually useful.

Like any metaphor, both "gravity" and "person" are/not true. They partly reveal and partly obscure human spiritual experience.

Beyond Metaphor Altogether

Spiritual masters routinely insist that the spiritual journey will take us through many different metaphors for God, and ultimately beyond having any images or metaphors all all. In an experience called "the dark night of the soul," God is said to disappear beyond any possible analogy or metaphor or human symbolic language for God. The unnamed, unnamable sacred becomes *not* like a person, *not* like gravity, *not* like love or compassion, not *like* anything that can be described in any physically vivid or emotionally rich human way. All possible statements about God fall silent in the face of this deep mystical encounter with the sacred. The light of intellect flickers and goes out, leaving only a luminous darkness in which even the familiar psychological experience of "presence" is absent. We can say nothing.

And I think—this is just a hunch—that both Jerome and the Septuagint translators recognized the continuity or convergence of Platonic mysticism with mysticism in the Jewish and later Christian tradition. After all, one can make no predicated statements about the Nous either. The light that blinds, like the fire we cannot approach, is a universal mystic image.

And in the aftermath of such experience, we realize yet again that even the most persuasive statements are wildly inadequate. By any name, God is beyond comprehension. And yet God makes all the sense in the world. Honest religion of any variety is perfectly okay with that paradox—and very careful about handling it delicately.

Finding God in Nature

Many people have always found the sacred most powerfully or easily discernable in wilderness landscapes or at least in scenes of great natural beauty. I admit that it can be difficult to feel any continuity at all between the sacred encountered in natural beauty and the sacred talked about inside dark and gloomy old church buildings. In many ways, as J. Philip Newell argues so eloquently in *The Rebirthing of God* (2014), Christianity desperately needs to reconnect to the sacred within the landscape. But "locating" the sacred in nature can also be disputed by pointing out all of the tragic, horrible, agonizing things that are completely "natural": tsunamis, hurricanes, tornadoes, gruesome parasites, terrible diseases, and above all the sheer fact of aging and death. If nothing else, our sun will go supernova at some point: for some people, that fact alone proves that the nihilists are correct in their cosmic despair.

Locating God "out in nature" may signify our sense of divine *absence* amidst the noise and congestion here in the city: the crowds, the anonymity, the hustle, the noise and grit, the anxiety of our ordinary lives. That's a serious spiritual problem. We need to be able to locate our own sense of the sacred amidst whatever counts as ordinary daily life.

What in the city reminds me of God or reveals something of God? Incessant traffic, perhaps. Beginning when I was eight, when one of Chicago's first expressways excavated its way across the block south of ours, I have never lived out of earshot of an expressway. At the moment I live half a block from one six-lane expressway and walking distance to another one that's ten lanes wide. Chicago is one of the nation's most congested cities—not New York, I admit, but crazy enough. And this is the city's single most congested neighborhood: gridlock is a daily event. More than once I have spent half an hour or forty minutes getting from the corner to our garage entry half way down the block. You want traffic? *I have traffic.*

Day or night, I have lived for almost my entire life with the steady hum of tires on pavement, punctuated by horns, and sirens, and the incessant clatter of demolition and construction. When I get up from my desk to pace, I watch skyscrapers slowly come down and slowly rise again, a process supervised by cranes whose heads rise above the landscape like brontosauruses in a swamp. (For some months, visible just to the right of my computer monitor, there was a bright yellow crane with a single large black eye. It peered in my direction across the roof of a slate-green building two blocks away. I felt somewhat sad when it rode off on the back of a flatbed truck.)

This is my landscape. This is the kind of landscape in which I have always lived. I probably do not understand what real silence might sound like. The summer after we were married, in lieu of the honeymoon we could not afford, we went camping. I had never been camping. I had never been in the woods at all. My mother disapproved of *picnics,* for heaven sake.

We settled into our sleeping bags. Warren promptly fell sound asleep, his breathing deep and throaty. I was kept awake all night by the terrifying, ungodly racket of what he later said were frogs. *Frogs?* It sounded like an alien army organizing itself for an attack on our campsite. And then, near dawn, a bear came through. It tripped on the lines holding up our tent, almost falling on top of us. Bears smell like greasy wool. I'd have screamed, but my throat was dry after listening to those frogs all night. All I could manage was a woeful croak of my own. Thanks, but I'm quite content with the sound of traffic.

God is like the sound of traffic. *My experience of God is just like that.* Just as I have learned to shut out the noise of the city, I have learned to shut out God. Just as I can hear the traffic if I stop to listen, so I can "stop to listen" for an inward reality as pervasive as the sound of tires on asphalt. I can, with sustained practice, get myself to something like a window. Holding it open for as long as I can, I can hear the hum much more clearly. It's "louder."

But it's there all the time, whether I'm listening or not.

Spiritual Exercises in Metaphor

Playing with new metaphors is fun. It opens us, I think, to advice from classic works of spiritual wisdom: we all need to unearth from within our personal histories an array of theologically inadequate images and metaphors for God. That's a very useful exercise: all of us inherit a variety of deeply problematic images for God: the patriarchal Heavenly Father, of course, and what I've been calling the Engineer Almighty. But there are other commonplaces: Mr. Sugar Daddy, Mr. Feel-Good, the Enforcer, the Distant Disapproving Parent, the Abuser, the Enabler, the Hypercritical Inner Voice. And cosmic malevolence incarnate, the felt experience that Somebody Up There Has It in for Me. We all know that perception.

It's also important to remember that we cannot ask whether the holy is or is not "out there" as something that "exists." That question is theologically mistaken from the outset: the divine cannot be defined or located vis-à-vis "there" or "existence" just as one cannot talk about a time "before" the Big Bang or a "place" where the Big Bang happened. The Big Bang was a physical event, they say (at least at the moment), and common sense insists that all physical events exist in time and space. But the Big Bang didn't. We have grown accustomed to the weirdness of such physics. Nobody bats an eye. Our cultural model for doing so is theology, which has long insisted that God is real although God lacks anything that we might understand as "location" or "existence" or other commonsense measures of "realness."

For example, Augustine of Hippo (circa 400 CE) sounds quite postmodern when he says, in one of his sermons, "What then, brethren, shall we say of God? For if you have been able to comprehend what you would say, it is not God; if you have been able to comprehend it, you have comprehended something else instead of God. If you have been able to comprehend Him as you think, by so thinking you have deceived yourself. This then is not God, if you have comprehended it; but if it be God, you have not comprehended it. How therefore would you speak of that which you cannot comprehend?"[1] In the end there is nothing we can say, including "there's nothing we can say," that will function success-fully in place of radical theological humility. As Peter Rollins wryly observes, we are driven to talk about that which remains beyond the reach of anything we can say. We cannot speak of God directly. We can only tell stories about our *experience* of God. These experi-ences are personal, partial, and culturally situated.

There is nothing absolute and unequivocal that anyone can say about God. God remains elusive, free to be what he will be, calling us beyond our comfortable concepts and beyond our comfortable slaveries into a future we struggle to imagine.

Spiritual Practice and Creative Practice

The rigorous and somewhat abstruse understanding of God I am describing here is properly called "apophatic mysticism." It is the extension into Christian spiritual practice of Jewish prohibitions against speaking the name or God or representing the divine in any visual art. As we are not to imagine God as a superhero, or an engi-neer, or sitting on a throne in the clouds, so we are not to imagine God by analogy to *anything* in our ordinary experience. The core spiritual practice here is mindfulness meditation, which I discuss in *Confronting Religious Denial of Science*, chapters 10 and 11.

1. Augustine, Sermon 2 on the New Testament, section 16, www.newad-vent.org/fathers/160302.htm.

As a practice, meditation has long been considered a threat to institutional authority and good order. It was denounced as recently as 1989 by Joseph Ratzinger, later elected Pope Benedict XVI.[2] For many of us, meditation practice has offered a profoundly healthy escape from excessive literalism, exhausted cliché, religious sentimentality, and so forth. Laying claim to the impersonal compassion of that which lies at the heart of human spiritual experience can be an essential step toward the deeper symbolic reality, which is that God is im/personal, personally present to us and yet simultaneously as radically remote from "personal" as one could possibility imagine. Both. Simultaneously.

Prayer, Art, and God

And consider this: artists describe settling down to their art in exactly same the way meditation teachers describe starting to meditate: the first step into the pure dark well of radical humanity creativity is to sit, center, focus, stop identifying with monkey mind, and so forth. John Main, OB, an incomparably important Christian meditation teacher, says it beautifully: "If we can resonate finely with the mystery, we are changed and enter another and more creative mode of being."[3]

Practicing presence in the here and now has always been recognized as essential to artistic production. Artists concentrate with remarkable intensity. But it is always an effort. Show up at the page, writers tell one another. Get into the studio. *Get your hands dirty.* Work as hard as you possibly can, but when necessary find the courage of the delete key. Start all over again tomorrow.

This resemblance between prayer practice and artistic practice has theological substance. *What are we turning towards* when we turn toward that pure dark well? *What are we turning toward* when we open ourselves to a surface that is without words, without

2. Ratzinger, "Letter to the Bishops of the Catholic Church on Some Aspects of Christian Meditation," October 15, 1989.

3. Main, *Monastery without Walls*, cited in WCCM.org "Daily Wisdom" of November 10, 2013, http://us4.campaign-archive1.com/?u=c3f683a744ee71a 2a6032f4bc&id=8b1c4bf60f.

images, without concepts, without even emotions like "love" or "presence" or "kindness"? *What are we turning toward?* Whatever it is, it is sacred. And it is generative: it is creative.

❧

Apophatic mysticism would insist that to say anything at all about God is to endeavor to say what we know we *can't* say. That is, in the end, an excellent definition of the predicament from which any of the arts arise. There is something that needs to be said, there is some *this is true* claim that needs to be claimed; but there is no ordinary language for it. And so we turn to music or painting. We turn to dance or sculpture. Or we turn to language that reaches beyond the limits of language, words under such pressure that they evoke more than they say.

That's where poetry comes from, and prose written with the density of poetry. That's where stories begin. That's why Christianity—and perhaps all religion—depends so centrally upon the arts that it ought to be regarded as itself an art, an art seeking to express something as profoundly central to the human experience as our capacity for sensory perception. At the center of all centers, there is not nothing. At the center of the center, there is a meaning that only imagination can begin to convey, and then only partially, only indirectly, only by evocation, only through the arts.

Prayer itself is an art. I talk about that at some length in *Confronting Religious Denial of Science,* chapters 8–12, where I consider what is intellectually offensive about prayer from a scientific standpoint. I'd love to repeat all that here, but there's not space. Here we are talking about God, and what is meant by God, and that's a question distinct from what is meant by prayer. Let's keep going, then, with the problem at hand: the theological "weirdness" of God-talk, which is that all God-talk is symbolic discourse because symbolism is our premier cognitive tool for grappling with paradox.

Whoever or whatever God is, God is profoundly paradoxical. What, then, can be said about God?

That's a topic on which arguments reach back thousands of years. Please buckle your seat belts and return your tray table to the upright and locked position. There may be turbulence ahead.

11

What, Then, Can Be Said about God?

If anything we might say about God we must simultaneously un-say, where does that leave me as a believer? Does my faith have no literal *content*? A God who is ultimately the Unknowable One might seem only nominally different from a God who does not exist at all. If that's the case, then the quantum turn I have described might seem to end up with an unbearable paradox that is minimally different from nihilism. I'm sure it will seem that way to some people. It doesn't seem that way to me, but I should explain why. What is the foundation of my faith? Where do I root myself, and how do my very human roots find water?

Here, in this: *I believe in God.*

That's a statement about me. It's not a statement about God. But it's the single most authentic, most reliable theological claim anyone can make. Do I *know* God in any intellectually rigorous way? Completely, unequivocally, with complete confidence? No. Not a chance. And that's not what I said. I said, *I believe.*

Let's begin with the word *believe*. Or, if you prefer, *faith*. The two terms have become synonyms over time, a convergence made more likely by the fact that "belief" has a parallel verb, "believe," but there is no verb that is parallel to "faith." If we had such a verb, I suppose it would be "faive." But we don't have that verb. And because we don't, English writers have turned to "believe" when they needed a verb to translate the verbs found in ancient creeds written in Latin. The absence of a verb form of "faith" has, in effect, been part of the pressure forcing "faith" and "belief" to function as synonyms.

But *faith* and *belief* are not actually synonyms, not exactly. Unpacking what the words originally meant is a useful approach to unpacking what I mean to say when I say, "I believe in God." So let's take a look.

"Believe" came into what eventually came to be called "English" after the Germanic Anglos and Saxons conquered England's native Celts in the 400s and 500s as the Roman Empire was collapsing and withdrawing troops from its far perimeter. "Believe" derives from a German word meaning "love."

If "belief" means "love," what does "faith" mean? When England was conquered again by the Norman French in 1066, "faith" came into English as a translation of a French word derived from a Latin word meaning "trust."

To say I *believe* in God, then, is to say that I *love* God. To say that I have *faith* in God is to say that I *trust* God. Love and trust, furthermore, are logically implicated in one another: to love someone is surely to trust them. And to trust anyone is surely to love them at least to some extent.

The slightly different meanings of *faith* and *belief* get muddled, however, when English translators needed a verb to translate the Latin verb *credo*. *Credo* is the opening verb of both the Nicene Creed and the Apostles' Creed: "I [*credo*] in God, the Father Almighty," and so forth. *Credo* is the Latin verb at the root of such familiar English words as "credible" and "credit." The word they chose was "believe."

That translation wasn't a mistake, mind you. "Credible" goes back to a Celtic word for "heart." Nonetheless, "credibility" has come to have an intellectual flavor, one having much more to do with adequate evidence than with personal relationship. When I say I love and trust God, am I necessarily saying that I find the creeds credible? That I accept the ancient-world creeds, and their innumerable descendants, as a *credible* set of lenses through which

I am to interpret both my own spiritual experience and the poetic nonfiction of Scripture?

Umm, no. Not exactly. We have other, and I think far better ways of explaining how Jesus is related to God, for instance, or what Scripture means when it refers to "the Spirit." Furthermore, the core of Christianity is what Jesus said about how we should live. It's not his metaphysical relationship to "the Father" and "the Spirit."

Christianity cannot insist that I accept *the literal truth* of ancient creeds as proof that I'm a "real" Christian. Accepting *the literal truth* of the creeds is not what it means to many of us to say, "I believe in God," or "I am a Christian." For a growing movement within Christianity, "being Christian" means endeavoring to live with compassion, generosity, and humble respect for the divine within everyone. It means greatest concern for those who have the least.

In an effort to make that fact clear, many dissidents have taken to calling themselves "followers of Jesus" or "red-letter Christians" or "followers of the Way." Those labels presuppose that everyone else in the culture knows what Jesus himself taught and what his Way entails. That's a dubious assumption.

And so I prefer "Christian humanist" as a label for us. As a label, "Christian humanist" gestures immediately to common ground with "secular humanist." As I explain in more detail in *Confronting Christian Absolutism,* chapter 3, Christian humanism is rooted in "the humane" as a moral standard and both rigorous scholarship and honest language as intellectual standards. "Humanist," like the parallel term "scientist," refers both to a set of skills and to a distinctive method of inquiry with its own implicit moral and intellectual standards.

"Christian humanism" as a label also has rich historical resonance. It goes back to the 1300s and to a distinguished set of public intellectuals and independent scholars (many of whom were also clergy). These were the men whose scholarship established the conceptual foundations of modern democracy. And so I'm claiming "Christian humanist" as a useful label for intellectually serious, theologically sophisticated, politically moderate-progressive, non-fundamentalist Christians.

It seems to me that the church cannot insist upon the *literal* truth of philosophical propositions from late classical antiquity. To do so is to obscure the encounter between the living God and living believers in our own day. Theological literalism is ultimately just as serious a mistake as biblical literalism. Churches that insist upon literalism are committing intellectual suicide. Irrationality is not a prerequisite for faith in God.

Christian fundamentalism will eventually die off: it is an aberration. Authentic Christianity will continue, reorganized yet again and from within by believers who continue to insist that the heart of Christianity is God and the human encounter with God. Period. *All the rest is commentary.* And commentary is to spiritual experience what sex ed is to sex.

It's obvious that I've read a lot of commentary in my day. (I've also written a lot about sex, for that matter.) It's also clear that I love and value commentary as much as anybody, and no doubt quite a bit more than most people. I've written the *Confronting Fundamentalism* series in an effort to demonstrate how much remarkable wisdom can be found in thousands of years of such commentary *if you know where to look.* But the fact remains that commentary is commentary. If I had to trade everything ever written *about* Shakespeare for the text of *King Lear* or *The Tempest,* I would do so in a heartbeat. I would also trade every page of every musicological commentary upon Bach or Ella Fitzgerald for any single performance. We need to keep our priorities straight.

I believe in God is a performance. Or at least it's the title of a performance: the performance that is how I live my life. It's how I behave toward others. It's whether I can turn the compassion and empathy I receive from God into a compassion and empathy that make a palpable difference in the lives of those around me. I am supposed to make that kind of difference to the people I meet because I'm supposed to know that the love God has for me God has for every human being equally, unequivocally, universally. I'm supposed to *feel* that. It's supposed to overflow from within me. *All the rest is commentary.*

Christianity is rapidly evolving. It will evolve more rapidly yet as the Gen X and Millennial generations come into their own as institutional leaders. I am old enough to see that clearly, and young enough to rejoice at the unforeseen adventures into which "I will be who I will be" may be sending us under this new generation of leaders. They are in many ways poised to achieve what many of us yearned for fifty years ago. They take for granted, with an easy shrug, positions and ideas that my generation fought hard to estab-lish—like the value of gender, racial, and ethnic diversity. That's now simply a given. They cannot imagine any other world. I *remember* another world. We stare at one another, bemused and affectionate.

This is as it should be: authentic, healthy artistic traditions evolve across generations. In literary tradition, for instance, at one point everybody is writing sonnet sequences, then suddenly almost no one is. For a while everyone is playing with the odd metaphors and scratchy, tweedy rhythms characteristic of John Donne. There's a civil war, and after the war every poet in England seems to be writing iambic pentameter couplets with the polished glow of pure silk. Then, just as abruptly, no one would be caught dead writ-ing couplets. Formal iambic pentameter dominates for centuries; it disappears; suddenly it's back, but in its return it is remarkably changed. The novel has evolved no less rapidly. Scholarly lives have been spent trying to explain how and why these "generational" changes happen and what sets them off. There is no explanation. There are major figures—Wordsworth, for instance, who defied the demand for heroic couplets and set the world to re-exploring Anglo-Saxon ballad rhythms. Shakespeare, whose dramatic mono-logues turned love sonnet tradition into a revolutionary vehicle for exploring the psyche. T. S. Eliot, who explored the dramatic poten-tial of the line break as an instance in the soul's debate with itself. There are examples like these of dramatic innovation. But there are no explanations.

Like literary tradition, Christianity has also evolved over time. No one has ever explained that either. But it happens. It happens because at its very heart there is the always unpredictable creative energy of moral imagination. Like God, the moral imagination will be what it will be, unpredictably.

The moral imagination links us in our own creative freedom to the creative energy that is God. The Gospels call that sacred creativity the *aionios zoë*, the everlasting life.[1] It is the vitality of the cosmos itself. It is a vitality that was here before any of us were born, a vitality that will continue after our deaths, a vitality that will continue even after the Earth itself is returned to stardust when the our Sun goes supernova.

I believe in God. I trust that "love" or "loving-kindness" or "compassion" is our best human equivalent or clearest human performance of this vitality—a vitality that my tradition warns me is by definition indefinable, beyond my grasp and yet, unfailingly, right here by my side.

I believe in God, and so the first news of the day is never the last word. Not for me. I trust that love and not hate is what's ultimately real. I trust that love in the end will endure beyond the endurance of hate, which in the end destroys him who hates just as surely as it seeks to destroy those who are hated. I trust that love can survive or revive in any of us despite the unspeakable agony that some people suffer in this life. As it is written: love bears all things, believes all things, hopes all things, endures all things. Love never ends.

And that is an inexplicable trust. That is a flat-out incredible confidence. To say aloud that I have this kind of confidence in the power of love demands from me an act of faith that is, in the end, a turning-toward, an inward tilting toward a light that I know by definition I will never understand much less explain to anyone else. In that turning-towards, I experience something that goes beyond "awakening," although "awakening" is a near perfect metaphor. "To awaken" is the proto–Indo-European stem behind the word *faith.* Its Sanskrit equivalent gives us *buddah*—the awakened one.

I'm not just awake. I'm alive, alive with the life of *aionios zoë*, the everlasting vitality that says to me, first and last, *be not afraid* and *you're not alone.* And in that courage, or at least in hope of that courage, I can dare on good days to be compassionate. I try to tilt the light toward others.

And that's faith, not fact. I couldn't prove it to you if I tried— and I'm not inclined to try. It's enough for me if you can imagine that when I say *I believe in God* I am saying that I'm working on

---

1. I discuss "everlasting life" in *The Confrontational Wit of Jesus,* chapters 7 and 13. The phrase does not refer to some five-star resort in the sky.

rustling up the courage to live like this. In saying, "I'm a Christian," I mean to say that I'm working on my own capacity for compassion. I'm working on my own capacity for generosity and the faith in abundance that generosity entails. I'm working on love and compassion because when I pay attention—on my awake days—I know that love is something stronger than gravity and wider than the wide blue sky. And I want to be part of it, even though I can't explain it, not even to myself. Love like that is beyond anyone's comprehension. We can't get our hands on it, not literally, not figuratively.

It doesn't bother me that I can't grasp it. I can't grasp how Shakespeare did what he did either, or Ella Fitzgerald, or whatever artist you want to name. (My current nominee for the inexplicable is Mavis Staples's performance of "You're Not Alone." There are musical intervals in her performance—intervals she bridges effortlessly—which as far as I can tell involve some inexplicable seventeenth dimension of musicianship. Maybe someday I'll figure this out enough to sing along, but I have my doubts.) I'm sure you have your own breathtaking nominees for the flat-out inexplicable. On a day like today, I'm inclined also to nominate the Georgia O'Keeffe clouds scudding softly through a blue sky, with their rain-dark bottoms and soft silvery tops almost blindingly bright in the angled light of an October afternoon. I can see those clouds over the top of my computer screen. Watching them, watching them distract me over and over again, setting my monkey mind loose, I cannot explain why I have spent my life writing *commentaries* rather than poetry.

But I was called to do this, protests some voice deep in my heart. God was crazy in calling me. I admit that. I'm a literary critic, not a theologian. I'm a poet. I resolved to be a poet when I was eight, when poetry first appeared between stories in the third grade reader. I vowed: when I grow up, I will learn how to make words sing like this. And I did. So what am I doing spending ten years struggling with God-talk, ten years of what Mary Oliver calls my one wild and precious life? *Ten years.* But God is crazy. Believers have been complaining about that fact for thousands of years. Call *me?* To do *what?* Are you nuts?

Maybe I'm the crazy one here. I'm taking a stand on that issue too when I say, *I believe in God.*

Just for starters, I use the word *God.* I don't write off this odd category of weird inward experiences, weird things people have done—like Shin and his cake. Or weird things people have said to me, like the choir master asking me what's a scholar like me doing in a *church*? Or things people have provoked me into saying, people like the colleague who took me out for beer and pizza one day. He did so to thank me—sort of—for sitting quietly next to him on the floor as he crouched under my office desk, coping with a severe flashback to devastating experiences in Vietnam. After far too much beer I heard myself saying to him that if I had any guts at all I'd walk away from my academic career to find some more socially responsible use for my talents. And he grinned at me with a wicked twinkle in his eyes, the angel of THE LORD incarnate, and he asked if I had such guts.

How could I back down at that point? Only God is that sleazy. So help me, only the Holy One can be that underhanded. Do not allow the Spirit of THE LORD to order a pitcher of beer. At lunch, no less. At lunch!

I know full well it is possible to explain away all of these moments as mere meaningless coincidence, or as my own unconscious stuff breaking through, or my own upbringing on the mystic side of Celtic spirituality, or who knows what. Endorphins. Briefly harmonic brain waves. Incipient schizophrenia, except I'm much too old now for that diagnosis. But for a long time I wasn't too old at all, and so I did worry about schizophrenia. Or the kinds of brain tumors known to cause religious delusions. Except that they don't remain essentially stable across a lifetime, which is approximately how long this has been going on in my life.

I know how easy it is to deconstruct all of these experiences, because over that lifetime I have deconstructed each of them. All of them. Repeatedly. Until I had to admit that I was expending remarkable energy over and over again insisting to myself *that was nothing.* That. Was. Nothing. Nothing, nothing, nothing. And whatever it was politely backed off into apophatic Nothingness. And then Nothingness hovered in all the same ways, like the white noise of traffic, like the nonchalance of gravity that's doing its thing whether I notice or not

I believe in God. God. Not brain dysfunction, not "unconscious material." God. It's as serious a word choice as any word I have ever chosen in a lifetime as a writer. God.

And in saying "God," I locate myself within a particular cultural tradition, a tradition called "Christianity," a tradition that at its best helps people to recognize and to grapple with such experiences. Surely by now, if I have convinced you of nothing else, I have convinced you that we need serious help from people who have spent *their* one wild and crazy lives learning Greek, Hebrew, and umpteen other languages, studying crumbling old scrolls, and reconstructing the ancient world in all of its amazing complexity. The church has its faults, God knows. But the church is also an archive of spectacular resources. I count among those resources the authors of books I have found engaging, the church musicians whose hymn choices can offer a wry interpretation of the readings, and the preachers of sermons that left me scrabbling madly into my purse for a pen with which to take notes. Or maybe for tissue to blow my nose. The structures and wisdom and teachings of Christian tradition at its finest have guided me toward sanity, safety, community, and wisdom I desperately needed.

The fact remains that every moment of my own experience remains eminently deconstructible. They can all be explained away. Any of them can be laughed off as plainly false, as meaningless, as trivial, and as not worth the weight I seem to assign to them.

That's the inevitable and necessary "not" side of the symbolic is/not. God is revealed to us *only* as that which is/not, and so any inward encounter with God can be written off in an instant if that's what you want to do. This too is taken to be a central fact about God. God does not force himself upon us. If God wished to be incontrovertibly evident, if God wished to rescue me and every other restless thinker from our own incessant questionings, God could do so. God does not. And it behooves us to remember this when we try to speak *about* God.

Only the arrogant forget. Only the arrogant pretend to have seen God face-to-face. Only the fundamentalist pretends to have grasped the "is" without any shadow of the "not," without any shadow of doubt, or humility, or diffidence in trying to talk about God.

As Peter Rollins points out so adeptly in *How (Not) to Speak of God* (2006), "ideology" and "idolatry" both derive from the same root, a word meaning something like "picture." Theology becomes idolatrous when it becomes fundamentalist—when speaks for God with sweeping certainty, when it claims to offer a complete and unquestionable portrait of the elusive Holy One.[2] As Richard Kearney argues in *Anatheism* (2010), God always remains the "stranger" showing up on the inner landscape of the mind. We always have to decide for ourselves whether to be hospitable or hostile—two words that despite their opposite meanings go back to the same root, a word that means both "enemy" and "guest." The guest/enemy, the is/not, to be fended off or welcomed. God? Or incipient schizophrenia?

How do any of us know for sure what to do with such experiences? For a long time I desperately wanted to know what to do. I wanted to know with deep intellectual certainty and unequivocal emotional confidence. Over time and with great difficulty I came to understand that such surety is not possible, a story I tell in *Motherhood in the Balance* (1999). We can trust or not, we can welcome these experiences or not; but we cannot know for sure one way or another what any of it means. The Holy One is inescapably elusive, as the wise have said for thousands of years.

No doubt some of what I take as significant religious experiences have been psychological artifacts of one kind or another. No doubt I have ignored visionary moments that I should not have brushed aside so nonchalantly. Maybe I will remember them later and reconsider. Maybe not. I'm sure I have failed to remember and reconsider what I blessed well ought to reconsider. *God is like this.*

I believe in God. I locate myself within a tradition and within a community that has long recognized the extent to which faith or belief is a creative process. Creativity is itself paradoxical. Imagination is perfectly spontaneous and yet entirely dependent upon concentration and focus. Creative works are deeply persuasive and yet a world apart from what is proven or provable. Creativity is intensely

2. Rollins, *How (Not) to Speak of God,* 11–12.

free and yet it produces the very most rigorous and durable structures humanity has ever created. That story about Moses and the burning bush dates to more than 3,000 years ago. The Abraham stories go back even further. Abraham, which means *Father of Us All,* and his wife Sarah, which means *Princess,* and their son, whom they named *Laughter.* And from them, the story goes, all of us are descended. We are the sons and daughters of laughter.

That sounds like a story worth telling, a story worth hearing. No empire has endured for half as long as that story. God-talk stories—in any tradition—are the most resilient things on earth. We are still enchanted by the Paleolithic cave paintings of Lascaux, convinced that they have a story to tell that we desperately need to hear.

I believe in God. I find myself loved and cherished and deeply known, known better and more clearly than I know myself. But even as I reach for that astounding affirmation, I must equally affirm that everyone and everything around me is no less deeply cherished. That includes polar bears on melting ice and chickens in their little cages. It includes both distant nebulae and neighbors with obnoxious yappy little dogs. It includes some child born this hour to a desperate mother who crouches, bleeding, in a fetid slum or a refugee camp or within earshot of bombs and gunfire.

I believe in God. I believe in a God revealed most clearly to humanity through just such an outcast child, helpless and homeless and impoverished. In the end, he gave his life in a physically courageous symbolic gesture asserting that God believes in us and God will never smite anyone. His mother stood with him to the end, we are told.

God believes in us. We are loved. We are trusted. We are capable of more than we dream possible. But the dream is ours to claim or not to claim. And some will call us crazy dreamers.

We must listen when they do so. The angel of THE LORD regularly shows up in the guise of unexpected people asking difficult and disconcerting questions. Maybe I *am* nuts. I must stay open to that possibility, or I risk turning the Elusive One into an idol of my own devising.

I believe in God. That is, in the end, all that can be said about God. As it is written, *I believe, Lord. Help my unbelief.*

Bibliography

Acemoglu, Daron, and James Robinson. *Why Nations Fail: The Origins of Power, Prosperity, and Poverty*. New York: Crown, 2012.

Alter, Robert. *The Art of Biblical Poetry*. New York: Basic, 1985.

Augustine. *Sermon 2 on the New Testament*. www.newadvent.org/fathers /160302.htm.

Bishops of the Netherlands. *A New Catechism: Catholic Faith for Adults*. New York: Herder and Herder. 1966.

Brown, Peter. *The Body and Society: Men, Women, and Sexual Renunciation in Early Christianity*. New York: Columbia University Press, 1988.

Confraternity of Christian Doctrine. *A Catechism of Christian Doctrine. No. 2. Rev Ed. of the Baltimore Catechism No. 2*. Patterson, NJ: St. Anthony Guild, 1941.

Crossan, John Dominic. *God and Empire: Jesus Against Rome, Then and Now*. New York: HarperOne, 2007.

Ehrman, Bart D. *God's Problem: How the Bible Fails to Answer Our Most Important Question—Why We Suffer*. New York: HarperOne, 2008.

———. *Lost Christianities: The Battles for Scripture and the Faiths We Never Knew*. Oxford: Oxford University Press, 2003.

Flinders, Carol Lee. *Enduring Grace: Living Portraits of Seven Women Mystics*. San Francisco: HarperSanFrancisco, 1993.

Howe, Marie. "Even if I don't see it again." In *Dancing with Joy: 99 Poems*, edited by Roger Housen. New York: Harmony, 2007, 146. This poem was reprinted with the title "Annunciation" in *The Kingdom of Ordinary Time*, New York: Norton, 2008.

Jenkins, Philip. *Jesus Wars: How Four Patriarchs, Three Queens, and Two Emperors Decided What Christians Would Believe for the Next 1,500 Years*. New York: HarperOne, 2010.

Johnson, Mark. *Moral Imagination: Implications of Cognitive Science for Ethics*. Chicago: University of Chicago Press, 1993.

Kaplan, Roberta. Sermon to Congregation Beit Simchat Torah, March 3, 2014. https://www.youtube.com/watch?v=U3mvEgzdITA.

Kearney, Richard. *Anatheism: Returning to God After God.* New York: Columbia University Press, 2010.

Kruse, Kevin. *One Nation Under God: How Corporate America Invented Christian America.* New York: Basic, 2015.

Kugel, James L. *The Great Poems of the Bible.* New York: Free Press, 1999.

Lakoff, George. *Don't Think of an Elephant: Know Your Values and Frame the Debate, the Essential Guide for Progressives.* White River Junction, VT: Chelsea Green, 2004.

———. *Moral Politics: How Liberals and Conservatives Think.* Chicago: University of Chicago Press, 2002.

Lakoff, George, and Mark Johnson. *Metaphors We Live By.* Chicago: University of Chicago Press, 1980.

———. *Philosophy in the Flesh: The Embodied Mind and Its Challenge to Western Thought.* New York: Basic, 1999.

Luhrman, T. M. *When God Talks Back: Understanding the American Evangelical Relationship to God.* New York: Knopf, 2012.

Main, John. *Monastery without Walls: The Spiritual Letters of John Main.* Edited by Laurence Freeman. Norwich: Canterbury Press, 2006. Cited in World Community for Christian Meditation, "Daily Wisdom," November 10, 2013. http://us4.campaign-archive1.com/?u=c3f683a744ee71a2a6032f4b c&id=8b1c4bf6of.

Martin, William. *With God on Our Side: The Rise of the Religious Right in America.* New York: Broadway, 2005.

Nietzsche, Friedrich. *The AntiChrist: Attempt at a Critique of Christianity* (1895). Translated by Walter Kauffman. New York: Penguin, 1959.

Newell, J. Philip. *The Rebirthing of God: Christianity's Struggle for New Beginnings.* Woodstock, VT: Skylight Path, 2014.

The Pew Research Center. "America's Changing Religious Landscape." Washington, DC: The Pew Research Center, May 12, 2015. http://www.pewforum.org/2015/05/12/americas-changing-religious-landscape/.

———. "'Nones' on the Rise." Washington, DC: The Pew Research Center, October 9, 2012. http://www.pewforum.org/2012/10/09/nones-on-the-rise/.

———."U.S. Religious Landscape Survey: Religious Beliefs and Practices." Washington, DC: The Pew Research Center, June 1, 2008. http://www.pewforum.org/2008/06/01/u-s-religious-landscape-survey-religious-beliefs-and-practices/.

Ratzinger, Joseph. "Letter to the Bishops of the Catholic Church on Some Aspects of Christian Meditation." October 15, 1989. http://www.vatican.va/roman_curia/congregations/cfaith/documents/rc_con_cfaith_doc_19891015_meditazione-cristiana_en.html.

Rollins, Peter. *How (Not) to Speak of God.* Brewster MA: Paraclete, 2006.

Schneiders, Sandra M. *The Revelatory Text: Interpreting the New Testament as Sacred Scripture.* San Francisco: HarperSanFrancisco, 1991.

Struck, Peter T. *Birth of the Symbol: Ancient Readers at the Limits of Their Texts.* Princeton, NJ: Princeton University Press, 2004.

Taylor, Charles. *A Secular Age.* Cambridge, MA: Belknap Press of Harvard University Press, 2007.

Underhill, Evelyn. *Mysticism: A Study in the Nature and Development of Man's Spiritual Consciousness.* New York: New American Library, 1974.

Wallace, Catherine M. "Coleridge's Theory of Language." *Philological Quarterly* 59 (1980) 338–52.

———. *For Fidelity: How Intimacy and Commitment Enrich Our Lives.* New York: Knopf, 1998.

———. *Motherhood in the Balance: Children, Career, God, and Me.* Harrisburg, PA: Morehouse, 1999.

———. *Selling Ourselves Short: Why We Struggle to Earn a Living and Have a Life.* Grand Rapids: Brazos, 2003.

Williams, Daniel K. *God's Own Party: The Making of the Christian Right.* New York: Oxford University Press, 2010.